W9-BTS-467

THE FREE PRESS

New York   London   Toronto   Sydney   Singapore

THOSE DIRTY ROTTEN

TAXES

THE TAX REVOLTS
THAT BUILT AMERICA

by

CHARLES ADAMS

A list of illustration credits can be found on p. 234

THE FREE PRESS
A Division of Simon & Schuster Inc.
1230 Avenue of the Americas
New York, NY 10020

Designed by Carla Bolte

Manufactured in the United States of America

10   9   8   7   6   5   4   3   2   1

Frontispiece: An engraving showing the Boston colonists dumping tea that was to be taxed by Britain during the famous Boston Tea Party. They were dressed as "Indians" to avoid repercussions.

Library of Congress Cataloging-in-Publication Data

Adams, Charles
    Those dirty rotten taxes : the tax revolts that built America / by
Charles Adams.
        p.   cm.
    Includes bibliographical references and index.
        ISBN 0–684–84394–3
        1. Taxation—United States—History.   2. Income tax—United
States—History.   I. Title.
    HJ2362.A3 1998
    336.2'00973—dc21   97-51744
                                                                    CIP

To Bill Archer, Chairman of the House Ways and Means Committee, for his determination to do what no modern nation has done—tear the income tax out by its roots. Even if he fails to do so, he will have started the assault, which will inevitably succeed, if not by us, then by our children in the next century.

Tyranny consists in the wanton and improper use of strength by the stronger, in the use of it to do things which one equal would not attempt against another. A majority is tyrannical when it forces men to contribute money to objects which they disapprove, and which the common interest does not demand.

—James Bryce, *The American Commonwealth, II*

Contents

Introduction

If you think you are mad about taxes, you'll be amazed at just how mad your forefathers were. The ever-increasing extension of federal bureaucratic power into everyday life has only been possible because of our tax system. Our excursion into Vietnam was possible because of our tax system. Indeed, our tax system has transformed our political and social order almost as radically as if we had introduced some form of Marxism.

Now that major tax reforms—real reforms—are in the forefront in national politics and debate, history should not be ignored.

At least until 1913, America was brimming with tax rebels. From the time when the British tried to tax us in 1764, to the adoption of the income tax amendment in 1913, our combative anti-tax character led from one rebellion to another. Many of these rebellions have been forgotten. Others have been misunderstood. Even the Civil War, the War for Southern Independence, was a tax battle going in both directions. Just recently the prestigious *American Heritage* magazine (June 1996) must have upset dyed-in-the-wool northern apologists with this comment: "The tariff, then nearly synonymous with federal taxes, was a prime cause of the Civil War." (Today's students read a lot about slavery, but when the war started, as a British observer noted, Lincoln "was prepared to give slavery more protection than ever before enjoyed." A more immediate problem was that the South was setting up a free trade zone that would have crippled northern commerce.) In large part the Civil War was an anti-tax "rebellion."

Throughout the first half of our history, Americans hated taxes with a passion, something they inherited from the founding fathers. A major tax revolt erupted within a matter of months after the adoption of the Constitution. Tax revolts died down only when taxes died down. In 1878, over a hundred years after the Declaration of Independence, and after the war taxes of the Civil War era had ended, *The Atlantic* magazine ran an article by Brooks Adams, grandson of John Quincy Adams and a recognized scholar in his own right. This leader of the most powerful political family in Massachusetts said, in "Abuse of Taxation":

> All taxation is an evil, but heavy taxes, indiscriminately levied on everything . . . are one of the greatest curses that can afflict a people.

In part, this book has been written to address the question of why the second half of our history is so different from the pre-1913 years. Can you imagine our current *Atlantic* magazine printing a statement like Brooks Adams's? Or the current leading political family in Massachusetts, the Kennedys, making such a statement? The editors of *The Atlantic* would probably get a call within twenty-four hours from the White House, the Congress, and the IRS Commissioner, wanting to know why such a prominent and respected periodical could say such a thing. President Clinton has even reminded us that we are an undertaxed nation, and should accept ever-increasing taxes on our labors.

But if you think Brooks Adams and *The Atlantic* were anti-tax, consider Thomas Paine. Known as the voice of the revolution, one hundred years before Brooks Adams, he called taxes "The greedy hand of government thrusting itself into every corner and crevice of industry."

In recent U.S. history, there has been a complete shift in public opinion about taxation. Despite the political popularity of tax cuts, most elites embrace a very different system from that preferred by Paine. Taxes are now beneficial and supposed to be looked upon with favor. The words of Justice Oliver Wendell Holmes, that "Taxes are what we pay for a civilized society," have been chiseled in stone over the entrance to the Internal Revenue Service building in Washington. Holmes even said that, for that reason, he "liked to pay taxes." But what kind of a civilization was he buying and at what price?

Throughout man's five thousand years of civilized life, civilization has been on the one hand uplifting, on the other cruel, inhuman, enslaving, and despotic. The ancient Greeks concluded, after looking over the civilizations of their era, that civilization and liberty were incompatible, since all civilizations operated upon despotism. And later, when Rome's civilization was in decline, one Roman remarked to his friends, "Let us flee to the land of the barbarians where we may live as free men." The trick of a successful civilization is to avoid crushing the creative wellsprings of liberty. Aside from authoritarian police states, the next most crushing mode of "civilized" oppression has been taxation.

By the mid-twentieth century, the American public had been so brainwashed about the virtue of taxation, and had become so ignorant of its true tax history and struggles, it is no wonder the statements of the founders and leaders in the nineteenth century seem strange, almost bizarre. But just about all of them, for well over a century, believed that taxations—except for the essentials of government—was nothing more than "legalized robbery," a phrase they used repeatedly. They were tax rebels with history on their side. For centuries, taxation had been a scourge for mankind. There were few moments in history when governments knew how to live on moderate incomes. It is true many of the world's political philosophers preached low taxation, but seldom did governments listen to them.

America was supposed to be different. It developed on virgin soil, and was not shackled to the political ways of Europe, where the divine right of kings and constant warfare made moderation in taxation and spending impossible. We succeeded in remaining free for 150 years. Much of this book, therefore, will focus on the pre-1913 battles.

There are five main periods of tax abuse, so far as the national government is concerned. Four of those periods produced tax rebellions: (1) the tyranny of British taxes, 1765–76; (2) the tyranny of the Federalists' taxes, 1791–99; (3) the tyranny of the tariff, 1828–61; (4) the tyranny of the Second Whiskey Rebellion, 1865–1900. The fifth period, the tyranny of the income tax, 1913 to today, began with the Sixteenth Amendment and the abandonment of all constitutional controls over taxing and spending. The first four tax tyrannies produced violence; the income tax tyranny, we can only hope, will end in a peaceful revolution. But if the historical anti-tax character of the early Americans reemerges, it may not be so peaceful. Governments should take note, and beware.

Considering the historical condemnation of income taxation except as a war tax, it is surprising that there has yet been no uprising against the current tax system. As I will explain, the reason is not hard to find: The initial income tax after the Sixteenth Amendment was class legislation against the rich. It was aimed at a small (5 percent) of the population, if that. It engendered a peaceful revolt of sorts. Many revolted with their shoes by leaving the country; others were able to avoid or reduce the tax by clever tax gamesmanship, which resulted in an insanely complex tax law. Then, during World War II, the tax enlarged to include the middle class, who accepted the hardship as a war tax. Somehow this wartime sacrifice carried over to the cold war. But the cold war is now over, and the historical need for heavy taxation is also over. The time for a rebellion is at hand, if taxes are not greatly moderated. The American people hate the tax and want to get rid of it, as polls conclusively show. If the long dormant, combative anti-tax attitude of our history resurfaces, the government will be in for a hard time.

Theodore Roosevelt observed that when there is "public excitement" over a political issue, there then will come those on the "lunatic fringe," who exaggerate the problem, distort reality, and endanger society. It is that type of personality that gave us the Oklahoma City bombing and the Unabomber. A recent novel, *Let Us Prey*, tells the story of massive bombings of IRS offices. Fortunately, it is fiction, expressing public discontent, but it is not inconceivable that some enraged taxpayer may take the author's imagination to heart.

Politicians, even the best of them, generally fail to sense the full feelings of taxpayers, and their potential for reaction. Margaret Thatcher was driven from office because of her attempt to put a poll tax on the British people. In Canada, the Progressive Conservative government, which had almost three hundred seats in the House of Commons, put in place a national consumption tax on top of the income tax. In the election that followed, they ended up with only two seats—the worst political disaster in the history of parliamentary government. The Liberal Party came to power with a promise to end this tax, but after a year or so they advised the people that they needed the money. Now, where do the angry Canadian taxpayers go? Both parties stabbed them in the back, so many migrated to the underground economy. The historically passive and accepting Canadian taxpayers have become tax rebels.

In America, President George Bush got his due for reneging on his "read my lips" promise in 1988. A protest vote for this breach gave Ross Perot almost 20 million votes and put an unknown, Bill Clinton, in the White House. How severe and how vicious must a tax revolt be for politicians to get the message? Time will tell; and maybe this study will enlighten one and all about the rocky road ahead.

I

THE TYRANNY OF
BRITISH TAXATION

1764–1776

*An unknown artist portrays the burning of
stamp tax paper in Boston in 1765.*

This fierce spirit of Liberty is stronger in the English Colonies probably than in any other people on Earth. . . . They are therefore not only devoted to Liberty, but to Liberty according to English ideas, and on English principles. Abstract liberty, like other mere abstractions, is not to be found. Liberty inheres in some sensible object. . . . It happened, you know, Sir, that the great contests for freedom in this country were from the earliest times chiefly upon the question of Taxing. Most of the contests in the ancient commonwealths turned primarily on the right of election of magistrates. . . . The question of money was not with them so immediate. But in England it was otherwise. . . .

The Colonies draw from you, as with their life-blood, these ideas and principles. Their love of liberty, as with you, fixed and attached on this specific point of taxing. Liberty might be safe, or might be endangered, in twenty other particulars, without their being much pleased or alarmed. Here they felt its pulse, and as they found that beat, they thought themselves sick or sound.

—Edmund Burke, addressing the British House of Commons on the eve of the American Revolution, March 22, 1775

1

The Roots of the American Revolution

The American Revolution is more of a mystery than most people think. The oppression and tyranny that caused other revolutions was missing. The Americans were not an oppressed people. On the contrary, they seemed the most blessed people on earth. They had the protection of Britain; they had recently, with George Washington as an officer, expelled the French from Ohio and Quebec, and thus removed any serious threat of French imperialism. There were jobs for everyone and opportunities for wealth based on work and merit, not birth. Their sons were not conscripted to fight wars in faraway places. Even the taxes the British tried to collect were to pay British troops stationed in America ostensibly to protect Americans. Moreover, in their charters, Americans were granted all the same rights as Englishmen. They were governed by the Common Law of England, and among other freedoms, were granted the right to a jury trial. They had local governments and assemblies that passed laws. In short, life was good, and if revolution is the consequence of oppression, then the American Revolution should not have occurred.

It is not unreasonable to wonder, were the Americans spoiled?

Did they not realize how well they had been treated by the mother country? Even the threepence a pound tax on tea that started the revolution was a pittance, especially by today's standards. The wanton destruction of the tea today would be considered the act of vandals and lunatics, not patriots fighting oppression. The colonists' moral and legal duty to pay some tax is difficult to refute. Many colonists remained loyal to the crown, and even after the revolution, long streams of wagon trains headed north to less hospitable lands in Canada, seeking a home under British rule. Their personal losses of lands, businesses, and property were enormous. Their exodus was a painful tragedy few Americans today know existed.

Many of Britain's leading writers found fault with the American rebels' cause and their secession from the British empire. Samuel Johnson, the master of English letters, had no sympathy for the Americans. His book, *Taxation No Tyranny,* set forth an impressive array of sound arguments against the colonists, and their rebellion over taxation. Said Johnson:

> The supreme power of every community has the right of requiring from all its subjects such contributions as are necessary to the public safety or public prosperity.

The truth of that principle, said Johnson, was as self-evident as

> that of obedience of children to the parents, and is not refuted by the assertion, that the consent of those who are required to contribute, is necessary . . . the far greater number of the subjects of England, men who are not freeholders, copyholders, who are a third of the landholders of the kingdom, and all women, were unrepresented in Parliament, yet were bound by laws enacted by the representatives of others.

Johnson proffered another cogent argument against the Americans. As a passionate foe of slavery, he pointed out the absurdity of slaveowners crying tyranny: "How is it," said Johnson, "that we hear the loudest *yelps* for liberty among the drivers of negroes?"

It should come as a shock—it did to me—that early in the nine-teenth century the Supreme Court accepted the British argument about taxes and representation. In 1820, the High Court was faced with the constitutionality of a federal tax law that applied to the District of Columbia and the territories (e.g., Michigan), when there was no representation in Congress. Surely, this was unthinkable in a nation founded on the battle cry that "Taxation without representation is tyranny!"

Amazingly, Chief Justice John Marshall had no difficulty with lack of representation in Congress. He reasoned, just as the British had in the 1770s, that Congress as a whole represented the citizens in the District of Columbia and the territories. But there were important distinctions, argued the Chief Justice, between taxation without representation by Parliament, and taxation without representation by Congress. There was a "vast ocean" that separated the colonies from Great Britain; there were "no common interests" between the colonies and the mother country; and eventually, the territories would become states and then they would have their representation. All specious arguments in the extreme. Travel to the District of Columbia from the new territories was just as arduous, if not more so, than sailing the Atlantic, especially later when Hawaii and Alaska became territories. There were innumerable common interests—language, trade, relatives, citizenship, religion, colonial charters, political leadership, and so on. And finally the argument that the territories might become states was a matter for the future. It took Alaska ninety years to become a state, Hawaii sixty years, and Utah fifty years.

This remarkable case, *Loughborough* v. *Blake,* is the most significant tax case in American law, although it is largely unknown and is cited only to show Congress' unlimited power over the territories. It is not just an unfortunate precedent but a tragic one, since it allows Congress to tax as it pleases while the Court looks the other way, in effect, tossing the Constitution out the window, as well as the main battle cry of the revolution. Once you accept the unbelievable absurdity that American law actually sanctions taxation without representation, it is easy to see how tax laws that flagrantly violate the Constitution persist to this day.

The real cause of the American Revolution goes back to the reasons the immigrants came to America. They sought freedom, yes, but not just any freedom. They sought freedom from taxation. As one Irishman wrote back home to Ulster in 1720:

> Tell all the poor folk of ye place that God has opened a door for their deliverence . . . all that a man works for is his own, and there are no revenue hounds to take it from us here; there is no one to take away yer Corn, yer Potatoes.

The Dutch came to New Amsterdam (New York) almost a century before, for the same reasons, as the 1630 pamphlet (opposite page) shows. It is entitled VRYHEDEN, the Dutch word for "Freedom." The pamphlet solicits immigrants for passage on a sailing ship to New Amsterdam, and the freedom it advertises is freedom from Dutch taxes, which at that time were burdensome, even crippling.

The Dutch had been carrying on a tax revolt against Imperial Spain for eighty years. It erupted in 1566, when the crown instituted a tax known as the "tenth penny." This was a 10 percent excise tax on everything. By 1630, the Dutch were soon to become a superpower, replacing the Spanish. But their dominance came at the usual price: They had to institute taxes.

When their freedom was finally won, heavier excises were in place that strangled Dutch commerce. William Carr, an English writer of some note in 1691, found it hard to believe that the Dutch would tolerate the heavy excises that were collected from the Dutch people.

Said Carr:

> Should we in England be obliged to pay the taxes that are here [Holland] imposed, there would be rebellion upon rebellion. And yet after

VRYHEDEN

By de Vergaderinghe van de Negenthiene vande Geoctroyeerde West-Indische Compagnie vergunt aen allen den ghenen / die eenighe Colonien in Nieu-Nederlandt sullen planten.

In het licht ghegheven

Om bekent te maken wat Profijten ende Voordeelen aldaer in Nieu-Nederlandt , voor de Coloniers ende der selver Patroonen ende Meesters , midtsgaders de Participanten , die de Colonien aldaer planten, zijn becomen.

Westindjen Kan syn Nederlands groot gewin.
Verkleynt syiands Macht brengt Silver-platen in.

T'AMSTELREDAM,

Voor Marten Iansz Brande Boeckvercooper / woonende by de nieuwe Kerck / in de Gereformeerde Catechismus, Anno 1630.

VRYHEDEN Pamphlet. An Amsterdam shipping company advertised for passengers to sail to New Amsterdam, promising freedom from oppressive Datch Taxation.

all that is here paid, no man may bake his own bread, nor grind his own corn, or brew his beer, nor dare any man keep in his house a handmill, although it be but to grind mustard or coffee.

Another English economic agent in The Hague wrote home, "a man cannot eat a dish of meat in an inn but that one way or another he shall pay 19 excises out of it."

From the British: No WOODEN SHOES

The excise, more or less a sales tax, was the primary tax throughout Europe, except for Britain, where there was an almost insane
hatred for it. When the British prime minister, Sir Robert Walpole, decided to cancel the customs on wine and tobacco, and replace the duty with an excise at the same rate, he set off a major tax
revolt. Excise houses were burned to the ground, mobs roamed
through the streets with placards: "Liberty, Property, and No Excise." Finally, he had to back down and went to the king and queen
offering his resignation, commenting, "I will not be minister to
enforce taxes at the expense of blood."

When news of Walpole's withdrawal of the excise reached the
people, there were celebrations everywhere. Church bells rang out,
bonfires lit up the sky, Walpole was burned in effigy, and in the
cities one could hear people singing ballads amid Dutch-refer-
enced shouts of "No excise, no wooden shoes."

When mobs were roaming the streets of London, protesting
against the proposed excises, one of Walpole's ministers proposed a
solution to Britain's revenue needs. He suggested that Walpole start
taxing the colonies in America. Walpole's answer should have been
considered by British governments thirty years later: "No, no; I
will leave the taxation of America to some of my successors who
have more courage than I have . . . I have old England against me;
do you think I will have new England do likewise?"

The caricature (page 11) shows Walpole in his carriage pulled by
a many-headed dragon, a common symbol of bad taxation not
only in England but almost everywhere at this time in history. The
tax dragon is devouring the wealth of the nation. A stream of coins
flows from one of the dragon's heads to Walpole, while the other
heads of the dragon devour the goods and wealth of the people.

Hatred for the excise was carried with the British immigrants to
America, who arrived almost daily. Walpole, says one of his biog-
raphers, "was in no way squeamish about the liberties of the indi-

Walpole's carriage pulled by the excise dragon, devouring the wealth of the people.

vidual or the privacy of a man's house." He introduced "savage punishments, and the full authority of the Crown to make the public conform to his system [of taxes]." Violence followed, and was, in the words of a recent biographer, "the expression of a profound and cumulative hatred of a system that seemed oppressive, tyrannical and corrupt [with power]."

In a tax dispute, taxpayers had little chance of success. "Once before the commissioners, the defendant had the cards stacked against him. He was guilty unless he could prove himself innocent." (Modern Americans could repeat this quote about the IRS too easily.)

Surveillance was also eerily modern. Candlemakers were rigorously watched. No one could make candles without informing the tax people of the time, place, and hours. Failure to report the exact number of candlemaking utensils resulted in a hundred-pound fine. Every month complete records of all candles had to be reported, and any broken candles had to be destroyed in the presence of an excise officer.

The bitter experience of the English with the excise tax found expression in the second most popular book among the colonists: William Blackstone's *Commentaries on the Laws of England,* in four volumes. Blackstone's treatise is still in print today and ranks with the greatest legal works of all time. In 1766, he condemned the excise with these words: "The rigor and arbitrary proceedings of excise-laws seem hardly compatible with the temper of a free nation." The Americans undoubtedly took note.

The colonists were also influenced by the tax struggle in Britain in the seventeenth century when Charles I was beheaded for instituting taxes the people didn't like. The first American settlers from Britain came from the turmoil of the British civil war, and they carried with them the ideals of the tax rebels, of Lord Coke (pronounced "Cook"), and especially the Petition of Rights. This petition was presented to Charles I in 1628, and required that taxes and a number of devious revenue devices (like forced loans, forced gifts, etc.) could not be demanded by any king without the approval of Parliament. Charles eventually signed the petition under pressure, but later instituted ship-money to circumvent the principle of parliamentary approval for revenue measures.

Ship-money was derived from the sovereign's right to impress private vessels into the service of the crown to repel foreign invasion. Elizabeth I used this power to defend England from the Spanish Armada. However, Charles used it to tax England by making a demand upon inland cities, such as London, no less, where there were no ships other than a few riverboats. Since there were no ships, Charles would take money in lieu of ships. And, of course, at that time there was no threat of foreign invasion, hence no real need. Naturally, that didn't go over very well, but Charles's court upheld his right to this levy, as he was the sole judge of any need. In time, this and a few other phony revenue gimmicks cost him his head.

The American colonists had every reason to believe that all the benefits of the civil war in the seventeenth century applied to them, for their charters guaranteed them all the rights of Englishmen—which meant they would be governed by the Common Law. They would have the right to a jury trial, the right of *habeas corpus* (protection from arbitrary arrest), and finally, they would have the right not to be taxed without their consent. This was the problem, because the colonists interpreted this matter of consent to mean local representation and local assemblies (their parliaments). So, a new twist developed in the interpretation of consent, which would produce a second civil war, this time in the colonies over the right of Parliament to consent on behalf of the colonists. Tax disputes in England had led to a civil war, and would lead again to a civil war in America. There had developed a long-standing English tradition that violence was the best way to get the crown's attention when taxes were concerned. Tax protestors had been violent protestors, and more than that, tax protestors were no fools, at least not when it came to the crown's search for new ways to drain money from the people's pockets. The colonist knew from centuries of English history that the rights of Englishmen were often illusory when the crown needed money. Let the government get a shovel in your money stores and there is no end to the mischief they may do to take the biggest scoop.

William Blackstone, in his *Commentaries,* had emphasized that at many times in English history taxes had been extorted from the people without their consent, and that the constitutional requirement of consent had been an illusion. The *Commentaries,* like so many English writings and histories at that time, contained extensive analyses of British tax history and tax abuses, which no doubt caught the attention of the Americans as the crown set a determined course to tax them. Still, American logic, at times, made little sense. A British civil servant wrote home from the colonies saying that if you approached an American about providing funds for British troops protecting them, he would respond with a "lengthy lecture on his rights." Chances are this lecture didn't make much sense, but the caricature of a taxpayer, burdened beyond all

British taxpayer with the yoke of innumerable taxes.

reason with a multitude of taxes, did make sense, and justifiable or not, this was the only truth that stuck.

From the French: THE DEVIL'S TAX SYSTEM

A French writer of this period said that if the Devil himself had been given a free hand to plan the ruin of France, he could not have invented any scheme more likely to achieve that objective than the system of taxation then in operation.

It was a system that produced the greatest viciousness between man and man, and man and state. It was a Devil's tax system to be sure, but not without parallels to other times and places. It taught the founders about the evils bad taxation will produce, not only in the injustices of government, but in the atrocities angry taxpayers are inclined to commit.

Violence plagued France over taxation for well over a hundred years before the revolution. Around 1705, Louis XIV's chief tax minister confessed to the queen that it was safer for a French soldier to walk through a Spanish village (France was at war with

The guillotine, where a large number of His Majesty's taxmen ended their careers, as enraged taxpayers used this bloody decapitator to vent their anger against the tax system. There were no tears when their heads flopped into the basket.

Spain) than it was for one of his majesty's taxmen "to pass from province to province in France—even to leave one's own house."

Unlike the American tax revolts, the French revolts were extremely violent, and often resulted in the lynching of a tax man, or even a suspected taxman. If life insurance had been available in France at that time, it is doubtful that a taxman could have obtained coverage at any price. The violence finally came to an end during the French Revolution, following the American tax revolts, when the entire tax bureau was herded to the guillotine and beheaded. No tears were shed when their heads flopped into the basket.

The slaughter of taxmen was indiscriminate. One of the leading scientists of that day was brought before the Revolutionary Tribunal for supplementing his income as a part-time taxman. He pleaded for his life, saying that he was a leading scientist and had much to offer his country. The Tribunal condemned him to death, answering his plea: "The Republic has no need of geniuses." The most important lesson the Americans learned from the French tax system—what made it the Devil's tax system—was the immunities from tax or reduced tax rates for some, while others were burdened with higher tax rates. No tax system could be just, so it seemed, unless the rates were the same for everyone. The root cause of the French Revolution and of so many of the tax revolts that plagued French society was blatant tax inequity. This lesson became of utmost importance after the American Revolution when the Americans were faced with the problems of establishing a new government, but hoped to cure the evils and perils of the European tax systems.

The colonists came from Europe, especially Britain and the Netherlands, and they brought with them vivid memories of Europe's tax follies. From the Dutch they knew that once taxes were in place, they could grow and multiply. Hence their fear of letting a government get its tax foot in the door. From the British they learned how a supposedly good government, with noble constitutional principles, could adopt brutal, burdensome taxes, enforced by savage punishments. A constitution seemed of little value and restraint once a government wanted your money. They knew that violence and civic disorder—murder and mayhem— would be the consequence of an unjust tax system. The colonists saw taxation as the root of most evil so far as civilized society was concerned, and they were determined, however naively, not to repeat European mistakes.

2

"There Were Giants in the Earth in Those Days"

—Genesis 6:4

There is no retreat, but in submission and slavery. Our chains are forged. Their clanking may be heard on the plains of Boston! The war is inevitable—and let it come!! I repeat it, sir, let it come!!!

—Patrick Henry, speech to the Virginia Convention, March 23, 1775

A British scholar, writing about the founders, said that never in the course of history had there been so many men at one time and place so skilled in the art of statecraft. William Gladstone made a similar comment in 1878: "The American Constitution is the most wonderful work ever struck off at a given time by the brain and purpose of man." It is no wonder that Americans have such a reverence for their founders.

The wisdom of these men grew out of the strife of the previous centuries. In England, a king had his head cut off over taxes. Under the strain of six major tax revolts, the great Spanish empire collapsed. Holland declined over too much tax, and in France, bloody tax revolts were everywhere.

No doubt the havoc bad taxation brought to Western societies stimulated men in that age to ponder the wreckage. They searched through history for taxes that had worked, and those that had brought disaster. They learned from the Greeks and Romans about the relation of taxes and tyranny, but they also spoke much about the relation of taxes and prosperity. It was, as now, no easy task to find a just and prudent tax system. Unlike today, they used history as their guide in their search for the best tax.

Using the ideas of the Enlightenment, our founders propounded the political concept of limited government and low, indirect taxes. That wisdom found its way into the Constitution. But somewhere along the way in this century these ideas were abandoned in favor of big, paternal government. We began to see no problem with big spending and big taxes. There were new tax philosophers, like John Maynard Keynes, who replaced the concept of low taxes and limited government with fiscal spending and taxing on a scale unknown since the collapse of Imperial Spain. Though great nations had taxed and spent themselves to death in the past, we thought that would not happen to us. After all, we had whiz kids in the Treasury and the Fed who would always keep the economy in good shape with fiscal gamesmanship.

It is hard to select from the great body of wise men who founded this nation who it was that contributed the most in his time, and for our time, to the revolution. I have selected three individuals from that period who I think contributed most, including one non-American who died before the revolution.

Thomas Jefferson has to be on everybody's list of the most important thinkers who influenced the new nation. He wrote the Declaration of Independence, and expounded repeatedly the right of rebellion and its necessity to keep government in line. Said Jefferson: "A little rebellion, now and then, is a good thing."

Jefferson's belief in the need and right to rebel permeated the

*Jefferson—who expounded the "sacred right of insurrection"
against bad government and bad laws.*

thinking of all the founders. They were, first and foremost, rebels, and had they failed, they could have been sent to the gallows as conspirators and traitors, as many a British politician demanded.

At that time in history, and for well over a hundred years thereafter, tax revolts were everywhere in Europe. Even the usually compliant Dutch finally had had enough by 1747 to start a major tax revolt in the Netherlands. Unfortunately, the Dutch revolt was about 150 years too late to save the declining Dutch empire. By contrast, what saved the British from the disasters of excessive taxation that had crippled much of Europe was the rebellious character of the British people. Scholars realize that the tax and fiscal policies of the British government were largely responsible for the rise of Britain to superpower status. But those tax policies were not the result of wise British politicians—they were the consequence of a rebellious populace that refused to tolerate excessive taxation, and didn't hesitate to burn down customshouses and assault His Majesty's taxmen.

As Jefferson argued, rebellions reminded governments of their follies. Representation was not enough. He wrote to Madison in 1785, suggesting that the country needed a rebellion every twenty years or so. He argued that governments should not punish rebels too severely for pointing out bureaucratic sickness in need of a cure. Rebellions, said Jefferson, were "a medicine for the sound health of government." He ended his letter with this Latin maxim: *Malo periculosam libertatem quam quietam servitutem* ("Rather a dangerous liberty than a peaceful servitude").

There were easily a dozen revolts in America and Europe in Jefferson's lifetime, and all of them were over taxes! This right of rebellion even found its way into the constitutions of some of the states. We find this provision in the New Hampshire constitution:

> Whenever the ends of government are perverted, and public liberty manifestly endangered, and all other means of redress are ineffectual, the doctrine of non-resistance against arbitrary power, and oppression, is absurd, slavish, and destructive of the good and happiness of mankind. (Article X)

In short, the founders believed in the sacred right of insurrection against bad laws, especially bad tax laws, and this belief was fostered by the remarkable success of all tax rebellions at the time. The excise revolts in England under Walpole were successful, as were the cider tax revolts in 1763. These revolts caused the crown to look to the colonies for revenue, and again there were tax revolts that culminated in revolution. Tax rebellions were common because they were successful. As the saying goes, nothing succeeds like success. And revolts are still ongoing today, though we revolt in less violent ways. We evade taxes and emigrate to avoid them. Violence may have ended, because the modern taxpayer has little chance of successfully rebelling against the modern Leviathan. Big Brother is watching and he is too powerful. Still, we are not complacent.

In Jefferson's later years, after serving as president and after reflecting on government's most difficult problem—taxation—he published treatises expounding what he believed should be the na-

tion's tax philosophy, in short: "Perfection of the function of taxation . . . to do equal and impartial justice to all." (1816)

Throughout this period, writing such treatises was a common
practice among statesmen like Jefferson, Madison, and Hamilton,
and it continued up until the Civil War. In one such treatise on taxation dated April 6, 1816, and entitled "Prospectus on Political
Economy," Jefferson set forth his principles as follows:

1. A tax should be so framed as to reach every member of Society, and "to draw from him his equal proportion of the public con-
tribution; and if this be correctly obtained, it is perfection of the
function of taxation." Jefferson is here agreeing with John Locke
and Adam Smith, that everyone should pay his proper "proportion
of the public revenue."

2. With respect to taxation, it is "the most sacred of the duties
of a government, to do equal and impartial justice to all its citizens."

3. He had no use for our current "soak the rich" ethos. Said
Jefferson:

> To take from one, because it is thought that his own industry and that
> of his fathers has acquired too much, in order to spare others, who, or
> whose fathers have not exercised equal industry and skill, is to violate
> arbitrarily the first principle of association, "the *guarantee* to everyone
> of a free exercise of his industry, and the fruits acquired by it" . . .
> extra-taxation violates it [a law of nature].

Finally, here are the words Jefferson wrote to James Monroe
while in Paris, June 17, 1785:

> . . . I sincerely wish you may find it convenient to come here. The
> pleasure of the trip will be less than you expect but the utility greater.
> It will make you adore your own country, its soil, its climate, its equal-
> ity, liberty, laws, people & manners. My God! How little do my coun-
> trymen know what precious blessings they are in possession of, and
> which no other people on earth enjoy. I confess I had no idea of it

myself. While we shall see multiplied instances of Europeans going to live in America, I will venture to say no man now living will ever see an instance of an American removing to settle in Europe & continuing there. Come then & see the proofs of this, and on your return add your testimony to that of every thinking American, in order to satisfy our countrymen how much it is their interest to preserve uninfected by contagion those peculiarities in their government & manners to which they are indebted for these blessings.

Jefferson could not have imagined, nor could he ever have expected, an American to move to Europe to avoid American taxes. It was of the utmost importance, said Jefferson, "to preserve uninfected by contagion" the American society—its laws and liberties. Today, of course, that is gone. In matters of taxation, most of all, we have been infected by European socialist tax and spending practices—and paid the price. Tens of thousands of Americans have moved to Europe to escape from a tax bureau known the world over as the world's worst in complexity, intrusions, and punishments. To try to stop this flight of taxpayers, Congress in 1996 passed a law prohibiting entry to former citizens who gave up their citizenship to avoid tax. It is ironic that at the time Jefferson wrote these words, more people fled from Europe to America to avoid Europe's taxes than for any other reason. Now the reverse is true.

IF THE FIRST GIFT to the founders from France was the example of what a good tax should not be—the Devil's tax system—the second gift was that great sage of the Enlightenment, baron de Montesquieu. In 1751, his book *The Spirit of Laws* was published in English and found its way into the libraries of all educated Americans. Studies now show that he was cited by more of the founders than any other writer. The Constitution owes a great debt to his philosophy of "moderate government" and indirect taxation.

The first observation of Montesquieu with regard to taxes and spending is that governments will misspend tax monies—a univer-

Montesquieu—the sage of the Enlightenment whose book The Spirit of Laws *inspired the framers more than any other political and tax philosopher.*

sal truth. In rather clever terminology, he emphasized that government leaders were most likely to spend money foolishly; that the public purse would be in the hands of profligates and spendthrifts:

> The real wants of the people ought never to give way to the imaginary wants of the state.
>
> Imaginary wants are those which flow from the passions, and from the weakness of the governors, from the charms of an extraordinary project, from the distempered desire of vain glory, and from a certain impotency of mind incapable of withstanding the attacks of fancy.
>
> Often has it happened that ministers of a restless disposition have imagined that the wants of the state were those of their own little and ignoble souls.

In other words, governments are often led by scoundrels and fools. On taxes, Montesquieu's principles were simple and realistic.

1. Direct taxes against the person were dangerous and were

natural to slavery; indirect taxes, as on merchandise, were more natural to liberty.

2. Excessive taxes would be evaded. But evasion would lead to "extraordinary means of oppression, and then the country is ruined." Both Hamilton and Adam Smith picked up on this in their writings. Evasion hurts trade and commerce, they said, and the government shouldn't punish the evader because the fault is with excessive taxation, not human weakness. The government creates the temptation, said Smith, and has no right to punish those who yield to it. If Adam Smith and Montesquieu were alive today, they would be first on the IRS's blacklist with red flags on their tax returns.

3. Excessive taxes deprive people of the rewards of nature for hard work and enterprise, and act as a disincentive, resulting in inaction, loss of jobs, and indolence.

4. Men living in a state of liberty tend to grant excessive taxing powers to their governments; excessive taxation leads to slavery.

Thomas Paine, like Montesquieu, had a negative view of government. So much so, he said, that when the people believe that government is "some mysterious and wonderful thing, excessive revenues are obtained." But to Paine, "When a government is just, taxes are few."

How important was Paine? President John Adams put it in poetic verse:

> Without the pen of Paine, the sword of Washington would have been wielded in vain.

Washington had Paine's pamphlets distributed to his troops, during winter quarters at Valley Forge. His most famous was *Common Sense,* which began: "Government even in its best state is but a necessary evil, in its worst state an intolerable one."

Paine described himself as champion of those "on whom the real burdens of taxes fall." His dominant theme was that taxes produce tyranny, which was a Greek and Roman theme. Revolution

Thomas Paine, whose pen was as mighty as Washington's sword.

was necessary, said Paine, to bring about a government "less expensive and more productive," which would produce an era of "peace, civilization, and commerce." In short, when a government is just, "taxes are few"; and "the enormous expense of government has provoked men to think." Today, we are rethinking government for exactly the same reason Paine stated—that our government is enormously expensive.

An overtaxing government was more dangerous than a foreign invader, said Paine, and a revolutionary change in government was necessary.

What has application today was his observation that there are two classes of citizens, "those who pay taxes and those who receive and live upon taxes. When taxation is carried to excess it cannot fail to disunite those two."

One cannot help but notice how right Paine was. In every effort to reduce spending today, there are howls of protest from those who live off the taxes of others. These people are well-organized and have good political connections and a substantial voting block.

But in recent times, taxpayers have been demanding relief, and they realize that relief can only come if those who live off the public trough find other ways of taking care of themselves. In short, a revolution in government, as Paine predicted, is necessary to produce a government "less expensive, and more productive."

Thomas Paine saw America as the land of liberty—because it was a land of low taxes. He supported this thesis with a comparison of British vs. American taxes (about 1792):

	England			America		
For a family of 5	£14	17	6	£1	5	0
For a family of 6	17	17	0	1	10	0
For a family of 7	20	16	6	1	15	0

Paine saw high taxation in European nations, unlike America, as a great evil, which he described in *The Rights of Man* (1791) as "The greedy hand of government thrusting itself into every corner and crevice of industry . . . [which] watches prosperity as its prey and permits none to escape without tribute."

That condemnation sounds more like the world's high income tax systems of today than those of two hundred years ago. With that inflammatory rhetoric against high taxes by one of the most popular idea men behind the revolution, it is no wonder violence erupted within a matter of months after the Constitution was framed, which led to a policy of extremely low taxation for decades to follow. America's tax rebels not only won the war against British taxation, they would also win the war against taxation by their own newly formed government, and that hatred would live on for well over a century.

Selecting Jefferson, Montesquieu, and Paine as the three leading idea men at the time of the founders was no easy task. Other readers may favor Madison, Hamilton, or a host of others who played no small role in the ideas that founded the new nation. There were the fire-eaters of that period, Sam Adams and Patrick Henry. There were those whose many pamphlets and "letters" set forth inspiring ideas that unified the colonies—that an injustice to one was an injustice to all. But Jefferson seems to embody the spirit of all the rebels with his appreciation of rebellion and his Declaration of Independence. It is interesting that when Lincoln gave his Gettysburg Address, his "four score and seven years ago" referred to that Declaration, not to the Constitution.

From Montesquieu came the ideas for the structure of the government, as well as the concerns about excessive government and excessive taxes. His ideas are as alive today as in 1751. Paine was an oddball. His pen may have been as important as John Adams said it was, and his ideas are as alive and compelling today as they were during revolutionary times.

3

"Perfect Nonsense"

No modern revolution was more deeply rooted in taxation than the revolt in the thirteen colonies. British taxes not only caused the revolution, but more important, they acted as a unifying force among the once disorganized and squabbling colonies. They rallied around the cause of taxation without consent, took up arms against the British, and finally formed the United States of America. The American independence movement was not deep-rooted; it began in 1766, when the colonial leaders met to protest British taxes under the Stamp Act. The Stamp Act Congress, as it was called, was the real birthplace of the United States.

The rallying cause of taxation without consent was at first a confused concept in the minds of the Americans. So much so, that the British chancellor of the exchequer, Charles Townshend, quite properly laughed at the position taken by the Americans as "perfect nonsense." This nonsensical reasoning made it difficult for the crown to know what to do. In the end, the Americans revolted when Parliament adopted the kind of taxes they said they would pay.

American merchants had been evading British taxes for decades.

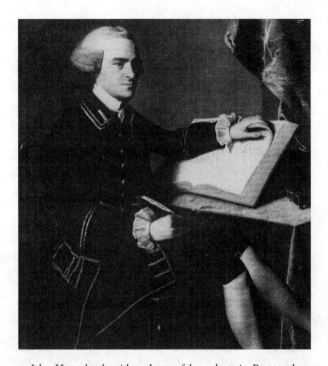

John Hancock, the rich and powerful merchant in Boston, the colonies' most notorious tax evader, wanted by the British tax ministry for evading what would be millions of dollars in taxes today. He enraged the British tax bureau by signing the Declaration of Independence first. and in a huge script, for the British to see, above all the other signers.

One of the worst offenders was John Hancock, who signed the Declaration of Independence in a large script to irritate British tax authorities. On one occasion, one of Hancock's ships in Boston Harbor was loaded with wine, but the ship's registry listed only a few cases. A suspicious customs officer boarded the ship to inspect the cargo. The crew locked him in one of the cabins. He later testified that for the three hours of confinement, he could hear the tinkling of wine bottles being unloaded.

Heavy taxes on non-British imported goods had been in force for years. They were not for revenue, but to protect the trade monopoly of British merchants and goods. Smuggling was everywhere, prompting one British merchant to complain:

The American derives his right of cheating the Revenue, and of per-
juring himself, from the example of his fathers and the rights of nature
and would continue to complain and smuggle, and smuggle and complain, till all Restraints are removed and till he can both buy and sell,
whenever, and wheresoever, he pleases. Anything short of this, is still
a Grievance, a Badge of Slavery.

Actually the British merchants had no right to accuse the American traders, as smuggling was more extensive along the coast of
England than in America.

Smuggling by the Americans centered on the Spanish, and this
trade was important because it brought Spanish gold and silver coin
into the colonies, which was badly needed for trade and commerce. The Americans had pleaded with the British over the years
to permit Spanish and West Indies commerce, and had submitted
petitions to the crown, to no avail. British merchants, with a monopoly on most trade, opposed any competition; yet the smuggling
trade was brisk, and in time the Spanish dollar became so prevalent
in the colonies that when the new nation decided to adopt a currency, they used the Spanish dollar, not the shilling, as their basic
coinage. Thus we can say that tax evasion, via the Spanish dollar,
gave us our present form of money.

To combat smuggling in England, the crown developed the
Writ of Assistance issued by the tax court. To obtain this writ, a tax
officer would swear under oath that certain taxable goods were in
a specific place evading taxes. The officer would then obtain the
assistance of a local peace officer and make the search. But when
this writ came to the colonies in 1755, the oath was dispensed with
and a tax officer, on his own, could execute the search and obtain
assistance from local police. An IRS summons today is very much
the same creature, issued by an agent without an oath or other basis
for legal justification.

In 1761, this novel form of the Writ of Assistance came to the
attention of James Otis, in Boston. He resigned as U.S. Attorney

General to challenge the legality of the writ. It had been issued to customshouse officers, even captains on British ships in and around Boston. Otis said he would accept no pay for his services. "In such a case I despise all fees." A young lawyer named John Adams (later president) sat in the courtroom and took notes. Otis argued for five hours: "the meanest deputy of a deputy's deputy, might enter any man's house or store where it was suspected contraband goods were concealed—a privilege in direct opposition to the cherished maxim that an 'Englishman's house is his castle' and is inviolate." Otis charged that the writ was "the worst instrument of arbitrary power, the most destructive of English Liberty and fundamental principles of law that ever was found in an English law-book."

Otis thundered that "An act against the constitution is void!" The judges ruled against Otis in typical tax court fashion that is still with us. Otis then went to the streets, and wrote a pamphlet against the writ: "If we are not represented, we are slaves." Protest began to appear in the other colonies, and colonial judges ignored signing the required initial approval for the writ. As it turned out, little abuse with the writ followed as the unsigned writs were left gathering dust in the chambers of colonial judges.

The Writ of Assistance was important in American history because its threatened use caused the framers to put the Fourth Amendment into the Bill of Rights, an amendment that was designed to protect taxpayers most of all.

The decision finally to tax the colonies for revenue came about because of the financial demands of the war with France. The British government was heavily indebted from that war, and the crown believed the Americans had benefited and it was only fair for them to shoulder some of the financial burdens. Furthermore, stories abounded about profiteering merchants in America and the free spending of British soldiers. To many in Britain, America was a land of milk and honey, lace and linen, silver and silk, paid for by the English taxpayer.

The Americans didn't see it quite that way. In their opinion, Parliament had done nothing to aid the colonists, except perhaps in Georgia, which was settled by paupers from debtors' jails in England, and had received some aid from Parliament. The other colonies, unaided and alone, had struggled during long periods of gloom and suffering. Of the vast sums that had been paid for expeditions, for land purchases from Indians, and for sustaining the settlers during times of famine and poverty, not one farthing had ever been given them by the crown. The colonists had built fortifications, raised armies, fought battles against the French and Spanish, without British aid or even appreciation. When the French and Indian Wars were raging, the Americans put up most of the men and money. By the mid-1760s, the Americans did not need, nor did they want, British troops in America. The war with France had been over since the Treaty of Paris in 1763. And that meant the right to tax was without justification on any grounds, unless, of course, the colonies were subservient to the crown.

In England, the people as a whole believed the crown had a perfect right to tax them, and to enforce collection with a vigorous hand. "Even the chimney-sweeps of the streets," said Pitt, the elder, in one of his speeches, "talk boastingly of *'our subjects'* in America." So the Americans did not have much support from the English taxpayer, who, like taxpayers in all ages, would have liked to find someone else to bear the burdens.

Parliament responded in 1764 with the Sugar Act, which was the crown's only successful tax in the colonies. Yankee traders in New England were the targets, and they protested vehemently, but the rest of the colonies showed little interest in their plight. Smuggling was open in New England and most colonists believed that the New Englanders were probably getting what they deserved. The taxes covered a wide range of non-British goods, with modest rates.

Protests against the Sugar Act were really directed against the

British periodicals didn't look upon the American rebels favorably. This London caricature shows some fiendish Americans with a tarred and feathered Loyalist, forcing him to drink tea with a rope around his neck.

administrative provisions designed to check evasion. Indeed, the American Revolution may have been more a response against British efforts to crack down on tax evasion than anything else. The act was a typical sledgehammer tax measure, which treated most potential taxpayers as crooks. A maze of regulations entangled all importers, even little coastal vessels. The personal chests of the seamen were seized if the contents were not listed on a customs declaration.

Besides the regulations, tax litigation was moved from local courts to pro-government Admiralty Courts in Nova Scotia. Civil actions against misbehaving taxmen were now forbidden (they still are), and informers were encouraged with a reward of one-third of the cargo.

The taxes from the Sugar Act were not as substantial as was hoped, and brought little relief to British taxpayers at home. In 1763, there were serious riots in Britain over new excises on cider. After tax agents were mobbed, the crown had the cider taxes repealed. In the search for new sources of revenue, the government turned again to the undertaxed colonies. The prime minister asked Parliament if any members questioned the right of the government to tax the colonists. There were no dissenters. He then asked if the colonies would refuse "to contribute their mite to relieve us from the heavy burdens we lie under." He even suggested that the colonies could devise their own form of taxation, but for the present the government would introduce stamp taxes.

Resistance to the Sugar Act caused the crown to bow its back, and at the opening of Parliament in January 1765, George III declared his determination to "establish *now* the power of Great Britain to tax the colonies at all hazards," and to "use every means in his power to enforce obedience in the colonies." At that time, he had the Sugar Act in mind, but the Stamp Act was also in the drawing rooms for submission to Parliament.

Stamp taxes were not new. They were invented at the turn of the eighteenth century and soon spread throughout the world. It prompted Adam Smith to remark in his *Wealth of Nations,* "There is no art which one government sooner learns from another than how to drain money from the pockets of the people." It was a kind of excise on written documents, newspapers—just about anything written on paper—and was popular in the colonies. As early as 1759, its use as a British tax on the colonies was proposed to Prime Minister William Pitt. He wisely rejected the idea, saying, "I will never burn my fingers with an American Stamp Act." By 1764, Pitt was out of office and a new generation of prime ministers took over, and now, as

Walpole had said thirty years before, they had the courage to tax the American colonies—and they got their fingers burned, to a crisp.

When the colonies learned of the Stamp Act proposal and debates in London, and when the act was finally passed in March 1765, to take effect on November 1, 1765, there were emergency sessions in the colonial legislatures, mob violence erupted, and pamphlets began to appear in the streets condemning the tax. Governors wrote to London advising that a rebellion had started, and there was no way the tax could be enforced. Most important, the Stamp Act united the colonies—something that had not been possible before, although there were attempts as early as 1754 when the First Colonial Congress was held in Albany, New York, with rather poor attendance. Now they had a common enemy, and the Massachusetts legislature proposed calling a General Congress of the colonies to remonstrate and protest against the Stamp Act, and also against the continued violation of their rights, such as the Sugar Act of 1764, which took away their right to a jury trial in tax disputes.

The call for a Congress fixed the first Tuesday in October for the meeting to take place in New York. While not every colony officially sent a delegation, all were present in one form or another. Nine sent delegates.

The delegates adopted a Declaration of Rights and Grievances, the main clause being:

> III. That it is inseparably essential to the freedom of a people, and the undoubted right of Englishmen, that *no taxes be imposed on them but with their own consent, given personally, or by their representatives.*

Specifically, they defined further that

> V. . . . *no taxes ever have been,* or can be *constitutionally imposed on them but by their respective Legislatures.*

Besides the declaration, there were three committees, each of which drafted an appeal to the three branches of the British government. There was an "Address to the King," which even suggested he could have the money he needed, provided he requested the revenue like an Aid in medieval times—as provided in Magna Carta. (At that time in England the king would call his Council of Barons and request money, called an Aid, for some specific purpose, usually a war of some kind. The barons would then debate the matter and decide if it was a worthwhile and reasonable request. Quite often, the king was turned down. On one occasion the pope had given the king some lands in Sicily, and he asked for an Aid to secure these lands. The council refused because "neither they nor their forefathers had done service in that land.") The problem with this revenue device is that they could say no. They spoke of the "invaluable rights of taxing ourselves, and trial by our peers . . . conferred by the GREAT CHARTER of English liberty." They repeated much of what they had proposed to the king in their Address to the House of Lords.

In their Address to the House of Commons, the committee members appealed to the commercial interests at stake, and they added that they did not want to send any representatives to the Commons from the colonies (where they would be outvoted). They referred to the English Constitution as the most perfect form of government, and they begged the Commons to hear their chosen counsel, Benjamin Franklin, in support of the petitions.

Franklin, who had actually applied for the job of selling the stamps, was a delegate for New Jersey, Georgia, and above all Massachusetts. Here are some of the questions put to him by the Commons and his answers:

Question: "What was the temper of America towards Great Britain in the year 1763?"

Answer: "The best in the world. They submitted willingly to the government of the Crown and paid, in their courts, obedience to acts of Parliament."

In Boston, a stamp tax appointee, Andrew Oliver, and the chief of police are seen being attacked by a mob. In the background is Oliver's new house, which was damaged. His effigy was hung on a tree with a rope around its neck. The next day he refused the appointment.

Question: "Did you ever hear the authority of Parliament to make laws for America questioned till lately?"

Answer: "The authority of Parliament was allowed to be valid in all laws except as should lay internal taxes."

What Franklin had done was to leave the door open for import duties by limiting his objection to "internal taxes," meaning that external taxes would be acceptable, in effect taking much of the punch out of the declaration and the later position that "Taxation without representation is tyranny."

Stamp taxes were internal taxes; external taxes were duties on imports. Below are the fronts of two pamphlets. One from Connecticut took a strange position in opposition to the Sugar Act (1764), arguing that if the tax rates were low (for revenue), then they were illegal; but if high (to prohibit trade), they were lawful. The other pamphlet on the Stamp Act appeared equally absurd, arguing that internal taxes were bad but external were good. Small

REASONS
WHY
The *BRITISH* Colonies,
IN
AMERICA,
Should not be charged with
Internal TAXES,
By AUTHORITY of
PARLIAMENT;
Humbly offered,
For CONSIDERATION,
In Behalf of the Colony of
CONNECTICUT.

NEW-HAVEN:
Printed by B. Mecom, M.DCC.LXIV;

CONSIDERATIONS
ON THE
PROPRIETY
OF IMPOSING
TAXES
IN THE
Britiſh COLONIES,
For the Purpoſe of raiſing a REVENUE, by
ACT of PARLIAMENT.

North-America: Printed by a North-American.
MDCCLXV.

Pamphlets

wonder that the British prime minister called the position of the colonists "perfect nonsense."

In the summer of 1765, there arose in the colonies a secret organization, the *Sons of Liberty,* actively opposing the act. They made all Stamp Act distributors resign their office, and they wrote and circulated hostile papers and pamphlets against the act, using a disjointed snake as their logo, which was designed by Benjamin Franklin:

The *Sons* often would parade through the streets, shouting, "Huzzah for Congress and Liberty." They assembled in New York in front of the building where the Stamp Act Congress was assembled and filled the air with a "New Song for the Sons of Liberty," in effect, their fighting song:

> A strange Scheme of late has been formed in the State
> By a knot of Political Knaves,
> Who in secret rejoice that the Parliament's voice
> Has condemned us by law to be Slaves: *Brave Boys!*
> Has condemned us by law to be Slaves.
>
> With the Beasts of the Wood we will ramble for Food,
> And lodge in wild Deserts and Caves,

Note the initials of the nine colonies that signed the Declaration.

And live poor as Job on the skirts of the Globe
Before we'll submit to be SLAVES: *Brave Boys!*
Before we'll submit to be SLAVES.

The Sons of Liberty carried placards on poles and stuffed in their hats, following the format of the British protestors a few decades earlier against Walpole's excise. This time they read: "Liberty, Property, and No Stamps."

There was considerable resistance in Britain to the logic of the colonists, who admitted that they were duty-bound to obey all acts of Parliament—criminal, civil, property, regulations of trade, contracts, etc.—and yet could disobey tax laws. This was amply ridiculed, as we have noted, by Samuel Johnson. His views, even today, have not been answered very well. Continued Johnson in his treatise, *Taxation No Tyranny:*

> Our Colonies therefore, however distant, have been hitherto treated as constituent parts of the *British* empire. The inhabitants incorporated by *English* charters, are entitled to all the rights of *Englishmen.* They are governed by *English* laws, entitled to *English* dignities, regulated by *English* counsels, and protected by *English* arms; and it seems to follow by consequence not easily avoided, that they are subject to *English* government, and chargeable to *English* taxation.

What seemed absurd to English scholars then, and now, is, how can you say you are bound by all laws of Parliament, except tax laws? In other words, you will decide what, if any, taxation you will pay, yet accept all other laws no matter what, and all the many benefits of British rule and protection. You can have your cake and decide whether or not you will pay for it, and how much.

Economics, not legal logic, brought about the repeal of the Stamp Act. Commerce suffered terribly; many merchants and shipping firms went broke. With repeal, there was jubilation throughout England as most British merchants opposed the act. There was an addendum to the repeal act that was to irritate the colonists. In effect, the addendum said that Parliament had the power to tax if it wanted to, and this was not to be interpreted as an abrogation of Parliament's taxing authority. Franklin said this provision would be no problem as long as Parliament did not try to assert it. A decade later, on the eve of the revolution, Franklin felt otherwise:

> But to remember to make your arbitrary tax more grievous to your provinces, by public declarations importing that your power of taxing them without their consent has no limits; so that when you take from them without their consent one shilling in a pound, you have the clear right to the other 19.

When the furor over the Stamp Act subsided, Parliament followed Franklin's suggestion and adopted a number of duties on imports from Britain. If the Americans foolishly believed there was a difference between external and internal taxes, the crown was willing to give them what they asked for, however absurd or ridiculous their reasoning might be. These new duties, said a member of the cabinet, "were perfectly consistent with Doctor Franklin's own arguments, while he was soliciting the repeal of the Stamp Act."

These new import taxes, called the Townshend duties, ran into some opposition in the Commons (the vote was 180 to 98). Edmund Burke, an extraordinary thinker in his day, argued against the new import taxes, predicting that the Americans would see the folly of their thinking, and would rebel over these taxes just as they did over the Stamp Act. Burke obviously knew the Americans better than they knew themselves.

Duties under the Townshend Act were charged on a few items: paper, dyes, glass, and tea. There were quartering provisions requiring the colonists to support British troops in America, indirectly accomplishing what the Stamp Act was supposed to do.

The Quartering Act was a disguised tax, but was tolerated except in New York, which had the largest number of British soldiers. New Yorkers refused to provide for the full needs of the troops and an enraged Parliament suspended the New York legislature and annulled any future acts. A hawkish mood developed in the British press. Said Samuel Johnson: "They are a race of convicts and ought to be thankful for anything we allow them short of a hanging."

The worst aspect of the Townshend duties was the establishment of a Board of Commissioners of Customs. Writs of Assistance were given to the board, and the arrogance of three customs agents in Boston played no small part in the eventual revolution. Said a prominent American historian, "Had it not been for the unfortunate personalities of Robinson, Paxton, and Hulton there might have been no revolution."

Canada might have stayed out of the conflict because of its superb governor, who refused to tolerate corruption and abusive misconduct by tax agents in his region. As it turned out, the revolution was probably more the consequence of the oppressive administration of taxes than the taxes themselves, despite all the talk about taxation and consent.

The Townshend duties helped the colonists clarify their thinking about taxation and consent. The Americans were not to leave the door open again. Distinctions between internal and external taxes were abandoned. Any tax required consent. Many British leaders agreed with the colonists. The former prime minister, Pitt

A British caricature shows the death of the Stamp Act, with British ministers attending the funeral.

the Elder, opposed taxing the colonies. But the best thinking came from Edmund Burke, who opposed any military action when war clouds started to form, saying, "People must be governed in a manner agreeable to their temper and dispositions."

The Americans finally realized that any taxation without their consent was against their disposition. Perhaps if they had taken that view in 1766 when they opposed the Stamp Act, an acceptable solution, short of war, might have been discovered. Unfortunately, the issue was resolved by following the example of the sixteenth-century Netherlands—war against the mother country that insisted on taxing them in a manner they didn't like.

An unusually odd caricature from 1763 helped fuel an uprising in Britain against a newly adopted excise tax on cider. The weird creature—An EXCISEMAN—appeared as a protest against the tax on cider. Violence erupted, excise houses were set on fire, and revenue officers were attacked. Riots were everywhere. As a result, the government repealed the tax because of the intensity of the revolt. This forced the revenue ministry to look for a new source of money to help defray the costs of the recent war with France (now settled). In their search for a replacement object of taxation, they

Exciseman: Could this caricature have led to the American Revolution? This 1763 cartoon set off riots throughout Britain over a newly instituted excise tax on order. The crown repealed the tax and in its place, began a program to tax the colonies.

made the decision to introduce stamp taxes in the colonies. The Stamp Tax Rebellion followed, eventually leading to the American Revolution.

But it was in Boston Harbor that the real quarrel with Britain began.

4

Vandalism with a Patriotic Fervor

The Boston Tea Party was the turning point in the struggle. Recently, American postage stamps have depicted the Boston Tea Party as a glorious act defying British taxation. Most people believe it was a protest against a tax on tea; but this is not the real story. The Tea Party is one of those myths that got started early in the days of the founders, and has become increasingly removed from reality. Consider this historically ridiculous cartoon of the nineteenth century, with crowds cheering on the docks as the phony Indians toss the tea into the harbor, with an American flag waving:

In opposition to the Townshend duties, American merchants had been boycotting all British goods. Some of the duties were withdrawn. The boycott focused on tea because for a number of years the colonists had been using smuggled Dutch tea. The British government decided on a clever scheme to deal with the tea problem. In part it grew out of an overabundance of tea in the warehouses in London. The government decided to sell this tea to a few pro-British merchants at very low prices, with a modest import tax. The final price would be so low as to drive Dutch tea off the market. It was believed the American housewife would buy the

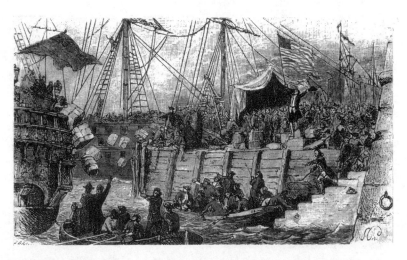

A historically ridiculous 19th century cartoon depicting the Boston Tea Party.

cheaper product, causing considerable financial loss to the Yankee merchants with the smuggled product.

It is not at all improbable that the tea would have been tossed in the harbor even if no tax had been imposed upon it. The merchants were not protesting against the three pennies for a pound of tea; what they were protesting is what today we call "dumping." It is considered an unfair trading practice for the companies of one country to dump goods on the markets of another country to harm local businesses. That is what provoked the merchants in Boston and elsewhere the most. The tax issue was a thorn as well because of the embargo against British goods that were subject to import duties under the Townshend Act.

This was really a big operation. There were seven large merchant vessels headed for the colonies; four ships for Boston, and one each for New York, Charleston, and Philadelphia. When news of the pending shipments reached the colonies, there were threats that reached the newspapers, commentaries by editors, and a general uneasiness and fear developed among the consignees. The importers in New York, Charleston, and Philadelphia lost their nerve, and the tea was sent back to London—tons of it.

A bitter potion, the Boston Port Bill (closing the harbor), is poured down the throats of the Americans from a teapot. The soldier has a drawn sword with "Marshall Law" on it. The "Boston Petition" requesting the recall of Governor Hutchinson lies trampled on the ground.

What also added fuel to the fire that followed was that the British government, the prime minister no less, was heavily involved in this whole operation, and it was his face that came up with egg on it when the clever tea game turned into a fiasco. That may explain why the British government overreacted to the actions of no more than sixty vandals in Indian costumes.

When news of the Tea Party reached England, public opinion turned on the colonists. Even America's friends in Parliament condemned the operation. The East India Company, which owned the tea, asked for compensation, but the British government reacted with fury. They closed Boston Harbor until damages had been paid for the tea, which was considerable, £9,659.

In defense of the Boston merchants, the implications of the underpriced tea were disturbing. If a monopoly could be granted for tea, it could also be granted for other products, and become a device to punish anti-British merchants and reward loyalists.

The Boston Tea Party is a sobering event that raises hard moral and legal questions. It is anything but the *cause célèbre* American writers have made of it. Benjamin Franklin was shocked, and acknowledged that full restitution must be paid to the tea owners. Most Americans believed this as well. Massachusetts was the seedbed of the hotheads who were constantly aggravating the British and local authorities. Unfortunately, the British government overreacted in typical sledgehammer fashion, as our government does over tax matters today. The Intolerable Acts that followed started the war. British warships and troops literally invaded the colonies. Oppressive revenue agents, no matter how abusive, were to appear kindly compared with fleets of warships

A LIST of the Names of *those* who AUDACIOUSLY continue to counteract the UNITED SENTIMENTS of the Body of Merchants thro'out NORTH-AMERICA; by importing British Goods contrary to the Agreement.

John Bernard,
   (In King-Street, almost opposite Vernon's Head.

James McMasters,
      (On Treat's Wharf.

Patrick McMasters,
     (Opposite the Sign of the Lamb.

John Mein,
   (Opposite the White-Horse, and in King-Street.

Nathaniel Rogers,
   (Opposite Mr. Henderson Inches Store lower End King-Street.

William Jackson,
   At the Brazen Head, Cornhill, near the Town-House.

Theophilus Lillie,
   (Near Mr. Pemberton's Meeting-House, North-End.

John Taylor,
   (Nearly opposite the Heart and Crown in Cornhill.

Ame & Elizabeth Cummings,
   (Opposite the Old Brick Meeting-House, all of Boston.

Israel Williams, Esq; & Son,
     (Traders in the Town of Hatfield.

And, *Henry Barnes,*
     (Trader in the Town of M   boro'.

A list of the merchants in Boston who continued to trade in English goods, contrary to the boycott called the nonimportation agreement. The Sons of Liberty distributed this leaflet to the populace on the streets of Boston.

and battalions of redcoats in battle array. Cannon, muskets, and bayonets replaced Writs of Assistance, seizures, and tax levies.

The Americans won the war after six hard years, because the British found the logistics of supporting troops three thousand miles away too burdensome. The American army was ill-fed, often poorly clad, and suffered a great deal. It was said you could follow the army in winter by blood in the snow from inadequate shoes, or no shoes at all. This ragged bunch returned home to bankrupt farms and governments. The burdens of taxation the British sought were a pittance compared to the taxes they now faced. If they thought taxation without representation was bad, they would soon discover taxation with representation was much worse.

The British learned from the war. In 1778, two years after the war started, Parliament, with the approval of George III, enacted a law which declared that no tax of any kind would be imposed on any colony for the purpose of raising a revenue. This wise enactment came too late. But for the rest of the British empire, the Americans had won the war for them as well. During the next 150 years, Parliament asserted absolute authority over all colonies, dominions, and provinces; but when taxation was involved, local assemblies of taxpayer representatives had to approve.

Though the colonists had won their cause, they had yet to learn that even self-government would not make the tax question easier. More strife was to come.

5

On the Horns of a Dilemma
(To Tax or Not to Tax?)

Even Napoleon was hobbled more by his own people than his enemies, since they too found taxes abhorrent. When he rode through the streets of Paris on his white horse, the citizens of Paris lined the streets, shouting, "Vive l'Empereur" (Long live the Emperor), and "Plus d'impôts" (No more taxes). Napoleon's most formidable foe, his indomitable foe, was not the British, but the French people, who wanted no more taxes. The heavily taxed French peasants and taxpayers thought they were fighting to end taxes—what their revolution was all about. Taxation became Napoleon's Achilles heel. He could defeat all the armies of Europe arrayed against him, rearrange the states of Europe at his pleasure, but he could not defeat the French peasants' belief that they did not have to pay taxes. They had won the revolution and destroyed the rich aristocrats who lived in luxury off the sweat of their brow. In the end, unable to develop an adequate tax system, Napoleon tried to conquer Europe, as the saying goes, on a beer pocketbook. Waterloo was inevitable.

The Americans had a similar problem after the success of their revolution. They thought victory meant freedom from taxation

Paper money issued by the Continental Congress.

from any source other than the state and local level. To submit to taxation directly by the Congress, an alien body far removed from the states, would defeat the very purpose of the revolution. But reality changed that illusion.

The colonists conducted the war through the Continental Congress, which became a joke by the end of the war. It went forward with a number of programs to rebuild the nation, even though it didn't have enough money to pay interest on the war debt or to pay for combat veterans. The paper money it issued became practically worthless, giving birth to the expression, "It ain't worth a Continental."

The Continental Congress continued as a very primitive form of government, and even before the Declaration of Independence it appointed a committee to draft Articles of Confederation to further define the structure of government. Finally, in 1781, the Articles were approved by all the thirteen new states, with only one primary branch of government, The United States in Congress Assembled.

The American rebels had fought the war to get out from under Parliament's power to tax, and they didn't want to create another parliamentary type of government to do to them what they had fought to avoid; consequently, the Congress could not tax but could pass tax measures with a supermajority, three-fourths vote. Once a revenue measure was passed, a requisition was made upon each of the states, dividing up the total tax bill by the value of the real property in the states. Personal property was avoided because of the slave problem, although twelve out of the thirteen states permitted slavery, but the heavy concentration of the slaves was in the tobacco and cotton states where slave labor seemed to work best.

In Parliament, of course, a simple majority could pass a tax law, and that was too dangerous, so the three-fourths approval meant that nine out of thirteen states must approve any tax for it to be valid. At the time, and even now, it is a very powerful check on too much taxation, or even discrimination in taxation, as well as too much spending. It is clear from reading the Articles what the founders had in mind.

The requisition system was summarized pretty well by the chief financial officer, Robert Morris: "The Congress had the privilege of asking for everything, but the states were given the prerogative of granting nothing." What money the states would grant, and when they would pay it, was "known only to Him who knoweth all things." Without money, the Congress under the Articles was like the Continental Congress, the laughingstock of the states and press.

Robert Morris was only one among an extraordinary number of brilliant leaders and thinkers in America. You could say that this was an age of political genius, and that genius gave birth to the United States of America. To keep the government afloat when the war was finished, he slashed the budget, fired personnel, cut costs, eliminated various government functions, and "thereby helped restore the credit of the central government."

Morris was well aware that the central government had to have the power to tax to pay its bills and pay the national debt. He viewed the debts incurred during the revolution as a blessing in disguise and a possible "cement to union," because these debts would eventually require federal taxes. Morris pushed hard for an amendment to the Articles of Confederation giving the federal

Robert Morris, chief financier for the revolution and Superintendent of Finance under the Articles. He waged a one-man campaign to grant taxing powers to the federal government, a kind of voice in the wilderness preparing the way for the new Constitution—years before others realized the Congress must be able to tax.

government the power to tax. He made an almost one-man campaign for taxing power: pressuring local authorities, writing pamphlets and newspaper articles, and using any other form of publicity. But all his efforts seemed to be in vain, until a handful of tax rebels lent a helping hand.

Meanwhile, the fiscal situation grew worse. Madison wrote in one of his private letters that he didn't know how much longer the central government could last. Debates over taxing power in the Congress got nowhere because of the requirement of unanimous consent for an amendment. There was almost unanimity over permitting import taxation, except for the opposition of that old warhorse from Massachusetts, Samuel Adams. He thundered that if Congress could tax imports, "every seaport, from Maine to Georgia would be filled with an army of overpaid excisemen, tide-waiters, and cellar rats. And what would the Congress do with the money? Would they dole it out with a frugal hand? No. They would squander it with a reckless profusion." Samuel Adams had thousands of years of history to back up his argument. There was little chance of any success in amending the Articles.

Eventually, in 1787, Congress called for a convention in Philadelphia to amend the Articles in what appeared to be a hopeless and futile effort. No one seemed interested in wasting his time, until a minor tax rebellion erupted in Massachusetts.

Massachusetts's debts, including the war debt, had reached such great proportions that high taxes had been imposed to obtain the necessary funds to repay the debts. These oppressive taxes ultimately resulted in an uprising known as Shays' Rebellion, led by an old war veteran, Daniel Shays. Thousands of farmers, armed only with pitchforks, rose up in revolt. They tried to seize a federal arsenal for real arms, but when two volleys of cannon were fired, the rebels dispersed and the rebellion ended. The press seized on the event and charged that the city of Genoa could defeat the armed forces of the United States. In response, delegates were sent forthwith to Philadelphia.

Like the Stamp Act, Shays' Rebellion brought the squabbling states together, this time to form "a more perfect Union." But support for a major overhaul of the Articles was not strong. When Patrick Henry heard about the meeting in Philadelphia, he remarked, "I smell a rat." And when the final document went to the states for ratification, it was a difficult struggle.

The delegates quickly abandoned any plan to revise the Articles. By 1787, there were no voices clamoring for the fiscal anemia of the Confederation. As much as everyone disliked the idea, Congress had to have the power to tax, but the question of fiscal controls was still an open one.

Constitutional restrictions and limits on taxing were not new. Many cities and regions in Europe enjoyed protection from different kinds of taxes. In Flanders, the French monarchy agreed not to levy a *taille,* which was an arbitrary levy by the king whenever he was short of cash. The same for the city of Saint-Denis (near Paris). Both of these regions enjoyed *taille* immunity in return for a commitment to pay a poll tax (head tax).

Restricting taxes was also achieved by restricting spending. In early modern England, a tax was illegal if the expenditure was illegal. For example, in 1497, Henry VII got Parliament to approve a tax for a military expedition against the Scots. A revolt erupted in Cornwall (southwest England) when collectors were lynched en masse. The Cornish people argued that the tax was illegal because the expenditure was illegal. No tax was justified for military purposes—except for defense. This view, as we shall see, found expression in the U.S. Constitution, but nobody ever took it seriously except Alexander Hamilton and a few Vietnam protestors. The latter refused to pay income taxes for an illegal war, and, as might be expected, went to prison for not paying their taxes, even though they had a very sound historical case for not paying.

The framers realized that taxing and spending are inextricably tied together, so you have to control both sides of the public purse—the spenders and the taxers. They would put clear-cut provisions in the Constitution to get the job done. If not, ratification wouldn't have had a prayer.

As expected, the very first power given to Congress was the power to tax, coupled with the restriction that taxes had to be uniform throughout the United States. This provision was to prevent any possibility of the new nation creating a Devil's tax system like the one operating in France at the time. Tax discrimination against some classes of citizens, and tax immunities for other classes of citizens in France, had kept the fires of rebellion white-hot, and would soon set off the horrors of the French Revolution. America wanted none of that. This caricature in Paris, 1789, depicts the French tax system, with its grotesque inequalities and lack of uniformity, the very flaws that the American uniformity clause was designed to prevent:

The debates at the convention and the writings thereafter show

In this caricature, the teeter-totter of tax justice moves in favor of the commoners against the low-tax, privileged classes. Justice with her scales has her foot on the teeter board on the side of those paying discriminatory high rates.

that the purpose of the "uniform" command was to prevent discrimination in the tax system. In the first draft on July 23, 1787, the clause read, "common to all." This meant, of course, everyone treated the same. Later, on September 12, it was revised to read, "uniform and equal," which was essentially the same thing. This final draft was then sent to the Committee on Style, which, strangely enough, dropped the phrase entirely. Madison then rewrote in the word "uniform," which is the way it finally read.

When the Committee on Style dropped the words "uniform and equal," was that intended to change the meaning? Apparently not, for this was a committee on style only. A prominent constitutional scholar explained it this way: "In providing for equality and uniformity they have done little more than state in concise language a principle of constitutional law which is inherent in the power to tax."

If uniformity was to require equal taxes for everyone, there was the need for additional protection when direct taxes were assessed. Direct forms of tax were looked upon as a great danger, as Montesquieu had warned, and the way to protect society from the tyranny that was inherent in direct taxation was through the rule of apportionment.

This rule in its best form was simple: the expenses of a nation should be apportioned, that is, divided up by the wealth of the nation. Adam Smith went so far as to say that the equality or inequality of a tax system is measured by its compliance with the rule of apportionment. Your share of the costs of the country (your taxes) is measured by your share of the wealth of the country—the same rule of law that applies to multiple owners of the land. The principle is still sound.

The obligation to allocate the costs of government on the basis of wealth had universal appeal to the founders. So much so that Thomas Cooley, the leading constitutional authority on the nineteenth century, said that an exaction that is not subject to apportionment is not a tax! What is it, then? It is an extortion for those required to pay more than their proportionate share. This view was also explained by another American writer, Benjamin Oliver, who wrote in 1832, extolling the greatness of American government:

> This right [property] is not infringed by equal taxes for public purposes, imposed by adequate legitimate authority. A misapplication or misappropriation of funds in the public treasury, however, must be considered a violation of this right . . . as it would be unconstitutional, therefore, to lay an unequal tax, as well as an act of oppression upon those who were compelled to pay the larger portion of it.

The apportionment principle ran into trouble at the convention. What about slave wealth? Wouldn't that wealth or property put an undue burden on slaveowners as compared to businesses on free labor? Of course it would, so the convention fell back on a bizarre concept—use people instead of wealth for apportionment and consider slaves as three-fifths of a person. It was a rough sense of justice as a tax idea. The framers destroyed the principle of apportionment as it had been expounded from John Locke to Adam Smith. What made it so outrageous was that the richest man in the nation would bear a tax burden the same as the poorest—the widow with a family of hungry mouths to feed. If there ever is a Constitutional Convention to revitalize the Constitution, and God knows we need one, that strange tax apportionment provision should be the first thing to go.

Direct taxes were looked upon with the utmost disfavor. In Madison's words, they were for an "extraordinary emergency." No one even suggested they would be a permanent revenue measure. James Wilson, who many believe was the real architect of the Constitution, said direct taxes would be limited to cases of "emergency." At the Maryland state ratification convention, a man named Alexander Hanson commented that direct taxation would be held in reserve, "nothing but some unforeseen disaster will ever drive them [federal government] to such ineligible expedients." Luther Martin, a delegate at the convention, acknowledged that direct taxes "should not be used but in cases of absolute necessity."

This universal fear of direct taxes was not just a view of Montesquieu; it went all the way back in history to the Greeks and the Romans, who taught that tyranny was the inevitable consequence of permanent, direct taxation. The great Roman lawyer, Cicero, went so far as to say that there should be no direct taxation unless there was no alternative other than complete national collapse. It is amazing that today, with 2,500 years of condemnation by civilization's greatest thinkers, we can find no fault with direct taxation, even in its most pernicious forms.

Today, neither of these taxing restraints has survived. The uniformity command is now an "empty shell," according to legal scholars, and the apportionment requirement was annulled with the Sixteenth Amendment. These provisions tried to protect us from the basic defect of democracy in taxation: overburdening a minority that doesn't have sufficient votes to protect itself.

The final protection from profligates was to limit the purposes for which tax revenue could be spent. Tax monies could only be spent to pay "the Debts of the United States," for "the common Defence," and for "the general Welfare."

Limiting military expenditures for defense only was in keeping with the Christian view that there should be no taxes for offensive wars. There had been a number of serious tax revolts in England in the early modern period when English kings tried to levy taxes for wars outside the realm—in Scotland, in France, even in Sicily. The Dutch and parts of the Spanish empire also held fast to this view, and there were many tax revolts in continental Europe against using taxes for military adventures.

Hamilton, in *The Federalist No. 34,* explained this as a "novel" provision in the Constitution, "tying up the hands of government from offensive wars founded upon reasons of state." But we must not prevent the use of the military for defense, said Hamilton, especially of our commerce. Hamilton's reasoning was not moral, but fiscal: America should stay out of wars because they cost too much. Not a bad idea.

The "general Welfare" restriction was designed to prevent spending for special interests—local benefits—what we call "pork barreling." In fact, most of today's appropriations wouldn't qualify under the general Welfare restriction. Like the "Defence" limitation, the general Welfare restriction has been thrown out the window, but for a while it almost prevailed.

When James Monroe was president (1816–24), Congress wanted to carry out some internal improvements, but President Monroe insisted they would be unconstitutional, as they were for local and state benefits. He then recommended that a new amendment be passed to give Congress the right to spend taxpayers' money for internal improvements. But with John Marshall running the Supreme Court, Monroe was persuaded that an amendment was not necessary, and after that, "general Welfare" became anything Congress wanted to do.

A much more fascinating story about the general Welfare restriction can be found in a biography of Davy Crockett. There was a fire in Georgetown, a suburb of Washington, D.C. Congress appropriated $20,000 to help the fire victims. Davy Crockett had voted for the expenditure. On returning home to his native state of Tennessee, and while out stumping for his reelection to Congress, he was confronted by an old-timer, who was extremely well respected in his district, over the $20,000 appropriation. He said he could not endorse Crockett because of this unconstitutional appropriation. He explained that he saw nothing wrong with the idea of helping the victims, but that it was not authorized in the Constitution, and Crockett had sworn to uphold the Constitution. Crockett listened to the old gentleman and realized he was right. He apologized, and agreed to tell his constituents at the next rally that he had made a big mistake and that he had no right to spend their money for anything unauthorized by the Constitution.

The general Welfare restriction on spending tax monies disappeared completely when the Republican Party came to power in 1861. Congress was no longer limited to the expressed powers listed in the Constitution, nor was the Tenth Amendment anything more than poetic verbiage. America had arrived at that sorry state of affairs in which there was nothing the federal government could not do as long as it invoked the appropriate constitutional loophole— loopholes never intended that were engineered by congressional lawyers with the Supreme Court's blessing. This is still true today.

The constitutional history of the United States is best illustrated in a story about the comedian W. C. Fields. A friend found him propped up in bed reading the Bible. "Bill," said the friend, "what are you doing reading the Bible?" Fields replied, "Looking for loopholes."

The expansion of federal power has had its most disastrous effect in what is known as "the supremecy clause," according to which all laws enacted pursuant to the Constitution are the "supreme Law of the Land." As long as Congress' power was limited to only some aspects of political life, the sovereignty of the states prevailed in all other spheres. But once Congress became able to do anything, state power became nearly meaningless, subject to the whim and will of Congress, and the federal judiciary. We don't have a federal government with limited powers, though the founding fathers intended us to. Instead, we have a national government in which nearly all sovereignty resides. There is no such thing as state's rights anymore.

When the final draft of the Constitution was submitted to the states for ratification, many of its authors were displeased with the document. Some of the delegates left without signing, and others had grave doubts about the final product. Even the philosophic Benjamin Franklin had his doubts when he signed. He left us these sobering words: "its complexion is doubtful, that it might last for ages, involving one quarter of the globe, and probably terminate in despotism." Still, he signed it, notwithstanding his doubts and apprehensions, and we, the inheritors of this flawed draft, are left with its pernicious loopholes.

II

THE TYRANNY OF
FEDERALIST TAXES

1791–1799

Alexander Hamilton, acclaimed to be "the right man, at the right time, in the right place" in American history. Yet his tax policies produced two significant tax revolts and brought an end to his Federalist Party and their brand of taxes in American life. Today, historians are beginning to realize he may have been more the wrong man than the right man when federal taxes are considered.

NOTICE

I do declare on my solemn word, that if such delinquents do not come forth on the next alarm, with equipments, and give their assistance as much as in them lies, in opposing the execution and obtaining a repeal of the excise law, he or they will be deemed as enemies, and stand opposed to virtuous principles of republican liberty, and shall receive punishment according to the nature of the offense.

—TOM THE TINKER, Pittsburgh, August 1794

6

Tax Revolts Against the Federalists

Jefferson didn't have to wait very long to see his theory about tax revolts come true. Within the first ten years of a Congress with taxing powers, there were two violent tax revolts, one of them very serious. It became obvious to Americans that taxation with representation could be just as bad as taxation without representation. The uniformity command turned out to be of little help, since taxes could be uniform in theory, but inequitable in practice. Rebellion was the outcome.

Alexander Hamilton became Washington's secretary of the Treasury. His appointment has been called "the right man, at the right time, in the right place," but it's doubtful that the farmers on the western frontier in 1794 agreed, and today, after two hundred years, scholars are finally agreeing with the rebels.

Hamilton followed Adam Smith's *Wealth of Nations* and persuaded Congress to adopt an excise tax on whiskey to supplement revenues from customs to help pay the war debt. Whiskey was, in Hamilton's view, a luxury. Furthermore, the nation drank too much, and so it was a health measure as well. Today, we would use the term "sin tax."

An exciseman being driven out of town on a rail after being tarred and feathered in western Pennsylvania, 1794.

There were two things wrong with Hamilton's tax. First, it was the hated excise—a tax which ranked first among the grievances that drove immigrants to America. A dictionary at that time defined an excise as: "a hateful tax levied upon commodities, and adjudged not by common judges of property, but by wretches hired by those to whom the excise is paid." To many Americans, even to the great patriots, Hamilton's excise was a betrayal of the revolution.

The whiskey excise ran into trouble immediately, for the second thing wrong with the tax was that money was almost nonexistent among the farmers on the frontier. Farmers used whiskey as money for trade. Grain was too burdensome to transport across the mountains to the east, so the grain was distilled into whiskey and transported to Philadelphia, where it could be sold or bartered for goods. The 25 percent excise in hard cash was outrageous; for these farmers, it was a tax on money and trade. By 1794, the entire region was in open revolt. Excisemen were tarred and feathered, just as British tax collectors had been twenty years before.

The hostility of the people to the excise is illustrated by the story of a local village idiot who playfully pretended to be gathering information for the excisemen. Rational men would have ignored this unfortunate soul, but angry taxpayers are often not rational or moral. The idiot was snatched from his bed at night, taken to a blacksmith shop, stripped naked and seared with a hot iron, followed by tarring and feathering. As one moderate expressed himself, "A breath in favor of the tax was sufficient to ruin any man."

The rebels were well-organized and demanded that Pennsylvania secede from the new nation. Liberty polls were erected as they had been in Boston to protest the Stamp Act. Revenue agents were called outlaws, and an oath was administered among the rebels, who called themselves "Whiskey Boys." The oath was to give no aid or comfort to excisemen. Local sheriffs who were foolish enough to accompany federal taxmen were seized, stripped naked, shaved bald, and covered with tar and feathers.

The whiskey stills of farmers who paid the tax were shot full of holes by a kind of Robin Hood who called himself "Tom the Tinker."

One observer on the frontier wrote:

> I have seen the spirit which prevailed at the time of the Stamp Act and at the commencement of the Revolution from the government of Great Britain, but it was by no means so general and so vigorous among the common people as the spirit which now exists in this country.

Civil disorder broke out when tax agents tried to serve tax summonses upon whiskey producers in western Pennsylvania. One such agent was met by a large number of people as he left his house. A knife was put to his throat and the people threatened to scalp and tar and feather him and burn his house to the ground if he did not promise to cease enforcing the tax. They ordered him to notify the tax authorities that his house could no longer be used as a tax office and he would no longer be in the business of enforcing the excise.

Another tax official, in Pittsburgh, having learned what was happening to his fellow tax agents, asked for military protection. Eleven soldiers showed up from a nearby fort. The tax rebels confronted the official and his armed guard. A skirmish followed in which three of the protestors were killed and four of the military men injured. The house they were in was set on fire and the tax officers and his armed guards surrendered to the rebels. The tax official resigned and left town. A meeting followed in Pittsburgh at which the question arose: were the rebels, in their violence against federal taxmen, committing treason? This concern not only cooled the rebels, it ended the rebellion.

In August 1794, in response to the certification by a judge of the Supreme Court that civil order had collapsed, Hamilton persuaded Washington to call out the militia of four adjacent states to make a show of force and put down the rebellion. But by then the rebels had decided the insurrection had gone too far, and most of them, fearing that they might have committed treason, punishable by death, had dispersed and gone home. Nevertheless, the army took to the field, with Washington in command, in full military attire. This was not necessary, as the rebels had already disbanded and gone home. But Hamilton wanted to go forward with the military operation and was at Washington's side in the field. Some face-saving was necessary, so a few of the rebels were rounded up and sent to Philadelphia for trial. Two were convicted and sentenced to be hanged. Washington then granted a full pardon to them, and a general amnesty for all the rest, and that ended the matter.

The final victory belonged to the rebels. Jefferson had the tax law repealed soon after his election, which ended the Federalist Party in America for all time. The farmers had argued that the whiskey excise lacked uniformity. Southern planters and other farmers were not taxed. There was no excise on cotton and tobacco, or other farm products. Should not these other farmers have also been taxed under the uniformity command? That argument was never answered; and it came up again in 1861 when the southern planters pressured their state governments to withdraw from the Union.

Until recently, textbooks have always praised the strong military action of Hamilton and Washington. But today, historians believe those books were wrong. Justice was on the side of the rebels, and

I DO ~~solemnly~~ promise, ~~henceforth~~ to submit to the Laws of the United States; that I will not directly nor indirectly oppose the execution of the Acts for raising a Revenue on Distilled Spirits and Stills, and that I will support as far as the Laws require the civil authority in affording the protection due to all officers and other Citizens.

September 11, 1794.

The amnesty agreement for the whiskey rebels in Pittsburgh. They promised to pay their whiskey tax and obey the law. Interestingly, they struck out the words "solemnly" and "henceforth" from the official wording.

the whole military operation was a political charade instigated by Hamilton to make a show of federal muscle. One recent historian noted that the Whiskey Rebellion had an important message for our time: "In 1991, as in 1791, tax resistance sends signals of popular beliefs about how democracy should work, signals that deserve reasoned attention."

Finally, the Whiskey Rebellion has an important history lesson as well. Here on the frontier of America a courageous group of citizens stood up for their rights against what was clearly an unjust tax. They capitulated in the face of a military encounter, and by the election process they accomplished their objective without bloodshed. The question remains, without the rebellion, would the tax have been repealed? Was the revolt therefore "necessary medicine for the sound health of government," as Jefferson believed?

The Fries Rebellion

No sooner had John Adams replaced Washington as president than another tax revolt erupted, this time among German settlers in eastern Pennsylvania. In 1798, Congress passed its first direct tax on lands, houses, and slaves. Under the Constitution, the tax was apportioned among the states by population. Houses presented a valuation problem, and assessments were determined by the number of doors and windows in each dwelling.

When assessors arrived to count and measure windows, the German settlers thought the government was about to levy the hated hearth tax, which was despised in Europe as much as the excise. The settlers organized into small bands, armed themselves, and scoured the countryside for assessors, who were seized, assaulted, and driven out of these counties. When some of the rebels were arrested, an auctioneer named John Fries marched on the courthouse and freed the rebels. President Adams, like Washington, called out the militia. Fries was arrested, tried for treason, and sentenced to be hanged. Fries asked the President for a pardon.

President Adams submitted to all his cabinet members a list of thirteen questions about the conviction of Fries for treason and his death sentence. The essence of his questioning centered on Fries' leadership in freeing local citizens who had resisted the enforcement of the new federal taxes. Was this not just a riot? Can mere resistance to the enforcement of a federal tax law be treason? Does not treason require an act of a military nature?

The cabinet was unanimous in its vote to hang Fries, but President Adams pardoned Fries nevertheless. The leading proponent to hang Fries was none other than Alexander Hamilton, who thereafter wrote a scathing attack on the president's final decision to pardon Fries. Hamilton noted that Washington had pardoned

Supreme Court Justice Samuel Chase, who was determined to send the tax rebel John Fries to the gallows for what was no more than a riot. Chase drove Fries' lawyers from the courtroom and forced Fries to defend himself. His charge to the jury was a railroad job unparalleled in American history. Unfortunately, attempts to impeach Chase narrowly failed, and to this day the people have no way of getting rid of misfits on the federal bench.

the whiskey tax rebels, and because of that there was now a second tax rebellion. Since Fries had also been pardoned, this meant that the government could soon expect a third tax rebellion. A third rebellion never happened, because these taxes and these tax rebellions sounded the death knell of Hamilton's politics and the Federalist Party.

The trial of John Fries was one of the most tragic blights on the history of American justice. Fries was represented by Alexander Dallas, a leading lawyer in the country, who became secretary of the Treasury under Madison. Justice Samuel Chase was determined to send Fries to the gallows, so he harassed Fries' lawyers to the point that they were forced to withdraw from the case, being unable to give their client a proper representation. Instead of ap-pointing new lawyers, Justice Chase had Fries defend himself—on a capital charge with no legal experience. Justice Chase's charge to the jury was a railroad job of outrageous proportions.

A few years later, Chase was almost impeached by the Senate for judicial misconduct and abuse in other cases. The impeachment, unfortunately, failed. Our current chief justice, William Rehn-quist, cites this failure as one of the great moments in America's history of the bench, making for an independent judiciary—mean-ing, of course, no federal judge can be removed, no matter how se-nile, incompetent, mentally ill, or, as in Chase's case, psychopathic. Not everyone agrees with the current composition of federal judges, appointed for life no matter how bad they are as judges. Any federal trial lawyer today will quickly acknowledge that the federal bench contains a host of misfits who produce a great deal of injustice, and strangely, as we shall see, in tax cases most of all.

Discontent against the tax policies of the Federalists was every-where, and the Federalist Party soon disappeared, as did its tax pol-icy, engineered by Hamilton. In the final analysis, it seems that Hamilton's taxes were not the right taxes at the right time and place. They were promptly repealed by Jefferson and returned only as war taxes in 1812, and again in 1861.

7

Madison's Problem:
What the Tax Rebels Were
Fighting For—and Still Are

The disastrous taxes the Federalists tried to maintain, and the
rebellions that ensued, suggest that the new federal Constitution was deeply flawed when it came to taxes. These tax rebels
were led by some of our greatest patriots, who soon dominated the
federal government for many decades to come. They became our
presidents, senators, and secretaries of the treasury, state, and war.
The Federalists were ousted on the grounds that their taxes violated the letter and spirit of the Constitution. Their demise came at
the hands of what became known as Madison's Problem.

I did not name Madison as one of the idea men behind the revolution. He was an idea man to be sure, one of the greatest, but he
was an idea man *behind* the Constitution. He is often called the father of the Constitution. He kept the only extensive notes on the
debates at the convention in 1787. And since the delegates decided
to destroy the minutes kept at the meetings, they are our only
record of the procedings. Because no official notes survived the
convention, the founders' intentions became lost, and over time
became malleable as clay.

When you study Madison's notes and his writings in *The Federal-*

ist, you don't sense any inspiration in the way the delegates debated and worked out compromises. They were hard realists, and had no illusions about what they were doing. They seemed inspired most by Thomas Paine's concern that government, at best, is a necessary evil, and they also realized that the greatest threat to good government and a free people was to be found in those who managed the government. Of course, they also endorsed Montesquieu, who acknowledged that bad government was the consequence of leaders with "attacks of fancy" and "little and ignoble souls." So the question became: How could they protect the people from such destructive leadership? Especially when it came to taxes?

Madison was not shy of confronting this issue in his writings to the people wherein he promoted the ratification of the Constitution. Here is the tax problem as Madison saw it:

> Yet there is, perhaps, no legislative act in which greater opportunity and temptation are given to a predominant party to trample on the rules of justice. Every shilling with which they overburden the inferior member is a shilling saved to their own pockets.
>
> —*The Federalist, No. 10*

Madison does not sidestep the problem, nor give it what we would call a "pat answer":

> It is vain to say that enlightened statesmen will be able to adjust these clashing [tax] interests, and render them subservient to the public good. *Enlightened statesmen will not always be at the helm.* (emphasis added)

Madison had obviously read his Montesquieu.

What, then, is the solution? Madison leaves the reader with this thought: "The majority . . . must be rendered . . . unable to concert and carry into effect schemes of oppression." Here Madison was focusing on what later became known as a potential defect in American government, what Alexis de Tocqueville (1838) and James Bryce (1888) both called "the tyranny of the majority." For Madison, this tyranny was most dangerous in matters of taxation, as he points out above. Granted, then, that they needed to prevent the majority from carrying out schemes of tax oppression, most of all, how would they do it? This was Madison's Problem, but it is our problem as well.

Madison and his fellow constitutional framers came up with two devices: First, in the Articles, they tried supermajorities, as we noted. Nine of thirteen states had to approve new taxes. This was a good tax-control principle, and today it has emerged in some states to check taxation, and even found its way into one of the proposed versions of the recent Balanced Budget Amendment.

But at the Constitutional Convention a few years later, they came up with a second device to prevent "schemes of oppression." Perhaps the supermajority was too much control, too restrictive of government. So Madison and his framers went back to a simple majority in the Congress for tax matters, but with the added restraint that not even a supermajority could overpower: uniformity for all taxes, and apportionment for direct taxes. A brilliant device to prevent "schemes of oppression." One of the strongest proponents of a stronger national federal government was Noah Webster (of dictionary fame). He emphasized to the governor of Pennsylvania, Benjamin Franklin, that "The idea that Congress can levy taxes at pleasure, is false, and the suggestion wholly unsupported." Why? Because of the constitutional restraints and limitations on taxmaking.

Alexander Hamilton was even more specific in his *Federalist No. 36*. The danger of "partiality and oppression" was prevented by the command of Section 8 of Article I, which provided that taxes "shall be UNIFORM throughout the United States." It is important to note that Hamilton capitalized the word "uniform," thus emphasizing the full and basic meaning of that term.

Five years later, in western Pennsylvania, grain farmers would wholeheartedly agree with Madison's and especially Hamilton's interpretation of the Constitution, and they would revolt and eventually make Hamilton eat his own words. His tax on whiskey would be limited to grain farmers. There was no tax on other farmers; hence this tax did produce "partiality and oppression," to

James Madison, the father of the Constitution, and the author of the idea that the majority must be rendered unable to carry into effect tax schemes of oppression.

use Hamilton's exact words. The revolt of these farmers was a fulfillment of Madison's concern, in which an inferior class in the nation was taxed while the predominant members, farmers elsewhere, were not taxed. This tax rebellion, like rebellions to come in the course of the next two hundred years, was rooted in the same problem.

The Congress has never hesitated to adopt taxes in which uniformity is sadly missing, and the Supreme Court has been more than willing to eschew its duty to enforce the Constitution with regard to taxes. Both bodies of the government, and even the president, have been delighted that Congress can now tax "at its pleasure." Thus Madison's Problem is still with us and haunts us even today. It makes tax rebellions, in one form or another, inevitable, as the victims of "partiality and oppression" rise up and revolt, take flight, or engage in fraud and evasion.

III

THE TYRANNY OF THE TARIFF

1828–1861

THE SITUATION.
OFFICER LINCOLN. "I guess I've got you now, JEFF."
JEFF DAVIS. "Guess you have—well now, let us Compromise."

A Civil War cartoon which promotes peace, a common philosophy through most of the North in 1861. Lincoln is a policeman seizing Jefferson Davis, who is holding the U.S. Treasury, symbolizing the taxes southerners were paying. Davis says to Lincoln, ". . . let us Compromise." Unfortunately, Lincoln never had any such intention.

The "Tariff" question, again, enters largely—more largely than is commonly supposed—into the irritated and aggrieved feelings of the Southerners. And it cannot be denied that in this matter they have both a serious injury and an unconstitutional injustice to resent. . . . All Northern products are now protected; and the Morill [sic] Tariff is a very masterpiece of folly and injustice. . . . No wonder then that the citizens of the seceding States should feel for half a century they have sacrificed to enhance the powers and profits of the North; and should conclude, after much futile remonstrance, that only in secession could they hope to find redress.

—*The Northern British Review,* Edinburgh, 1862

8

The Abominable Tariff

The American people used the ballot box to oust the Federalist Party and the taxes they tried to institute. Their taxes were repealed, and their bureaucracy (the forerunner of the IRS) dismantled. Except for import duties, all other federal taxes disappeared. They reappeared for a short season after the War of 1812, but again, they did not last long.

From 1800 to 1861, taxes took on a different character, not so much in how they were raised but with regard to their effect on manufacturing. The country was in its commercial infancy, and it was popular to adopt protective tariffs so local businesses would not be destroyed by competition from Europe. The first such tariff had substantial support around the nation, even in the South, but by the 1820s, southern planters began to see the tariff as an unjust, even unconstitutional tax. The 1828 tariff, which was the highest in history, was called the "Tariff of Abomination." Southerners wanted an open market for manufactured goods; northerners wanted an exclusive market, rid of foreign competition. The high tariff forced the southerners either to buy northern goods at inflated prices, or to buy highly taxed imports that went to enrich northern coffers. This, southerners claimed, made the tax system unfair, and hence unconstitutional. A just tax meant every region would pay its share. Under the so-called Tariff of Abomination, southerners claimed they were paying the lion's share.

The 1832 tariff, which reduced taxes somewhat, but not enough for South Carolina, elicited a hostile reaction that produced the first serious constitutional crisis since Hamilton's taxes. South Carolina nullified both tariffs—1828 and 1832—on the grounds that they were unconstitutional. This was not an inappropriate response. Nullification had a long and respectable history. It was proposed by Jefferson, and in 1832 it was widely believed that the federal government could not breach the Constitution or exceed the powers the states had given to it. If it did so, any state had the right to nullify the unconstitutional act. The practice was not just southern. A number of northern states, right up until the Civil War, nullified federal laws, most often the Fugitive Slave Act. Northern states went so far as to enact harsh criminal fines and prison terms for anyone enforcing that federal law.

President Andrew Jackson responded strongly to the nullification of the tariffs of 1828 and 1832. He threatened military action and treason charges against any person resisting the enforcement of the tariff. In this standoff, a compromise was reached by lowering the tariff and avoiding civil strife. Indignation against the tariff continued throughout the South, notwithstanding the moderate tariffs that were adopted thereafter up until 1861. Talk of secession as a defense against high tariffs found expression from many leaders in the South, John C. Calhoun being the most prominent.

In 1850, when Calhoun was dying, he made a reply in the Senate to Daniel Webster on the Union. He was too ill to attend the session, but he had his address read to the senators in chambers. He reiterated the grievances of the South: the exclusion of the South from new territories and the growing dominance of the North in national politics. Calhoun was concerned with the replacement of our federal republic, as originally intended by the framers, with "a great national consolidated democracy." But his complaint about northern tax policy, the high tariff, was what struck home for most southerners. According to Calhoun, the North had adopted

A system of revenue and disbursements, in which an undue proportion of the burden of taxation has been imposed upon the South, and an undue proportion of its proceeds appropriated to the North . . . duties must necessarily fall mainly on the exporting States, and the South, as the great exporting portion of the Union, has in reality paid vastly more than her due proportion of the revenue.

Note Calhoun's liberal use of the term "proportion." This was the critical word and the echo of the by now entrenched idea that taxes in order to be just taxes had to be proportionate throughout the country, and among taxpayers. Lacking that essential quality, the tariff, in effect, lacked uniformity, and that was the basis of the South's argument that it was unconstitutional.

Protecting infant industries was not the only reason given for a high tariff. Lincoln reasoned that free trade, or low tariffs, "must result in the increase in both useless labour, and idleness; and so, in proportion, must produce want and ruin among our people." This seems a specious argument at best. Between the North's arguments for a high tariff and the South's arguments for a low tariff, there seemed to be no middle ground. If the South had remained free trade, and the North high tariff, northern business and commerce would have suffered considerably, perhaps catastrophically. With northern tariffs, the South would have suffered equally.

9

The "Other" Great Debate

The tariff, then nearly synonymous with federal
taxes, was a prime cause of the Civil War.

—*American Heritage,* June 1996

The great debates over the cause of the Civil War, or the War for Southern Independence, have been going on ever since British writers probed the cause of the "American Conflict" in 1861. Myriad interpretations have arisen since then. "Cause" is a slippery word. Some blamed the war on the cotton gin, others on old enemies in the English civil war—Puritans in the North and Royalists in the South. Today, most students of American history are still taught that slavery was the real cause. Unfortunately, that interpretation is only partly true.

By 1860, hatreds bred in the revolution had long since disappeared. On the contrary, the British were troubled by the American Civil War. In 1861, one British publication called it a "catastrophe too fresh, too sudden and too terrible in its consequences." It was "the calamity of a people who are our kinsmen by

John Stuart Mill
"That creature Dickens"

blood, who speak the same tongue and inherit the glories of a common literature."

John Stuart Mill vs. Charles Dickens

Interestingly, it is in a debate between two famous Britons that we find one of the most incisive commentaries on the cause of the American Civil War. Charles Dickens and John Stuart Mill had been carrying on a war of words for over a decade. When Mill wrote his famous *Political Economy* (1848), Dickens responded with two novels, first *Bleak House* (1852), and then *Hard Times.* The latter novel, according to historians, "manhandled" Mill's treatise. An enraged Mill wrote, after reading *Bleak House,* that "that creature Dickens" was filled with "vulgar impudence," and his writings were "extremely repugnant to me."

This long-standing feud between Dickens and Mill found new expression in their views on the American conflict. Mill was an aristocrat and should have had little trouble identifying with south-

Charles Dickens
Slavery? Ah, humbug!

ern culture, but instead he railed against it vociferously, while responding to one of Dickens' articles about the cause of the War.

The Opening Argument: SLAVERY? AH, HUMBUG!

Dickens was active in contemporary affairs and acted as editor of a weekly periodical, *All the Year Round,* that had started in 1859 and continued weekly for almost two decades after his death. He was its primary contributor.

He wrote two articles on the American war. The first, dated December 21, 1861, argued that the "cause of the disruption" was not slavery.

Dickens pointed out that the Constitution of the United States was written by slaveholders. Of the thirteen states, twelve permitted slavery in 1781. So, from the beginning, argued Dickens, the issue was never slavery. It was the woes of state-building that surfaced inevitably. After all, Jefferson and Washington had predicted that the Union would come to blows with itself simply because of its growing size. Those blows, economic more than social, surfaced naturally between North and South.

As Dickens wrote:

The struggle between North and South has been of long duration. The South having the lead in the federation had fought some hard political battles to retain it. . . . But in the last presidential election, which was a trial of strength between South and North, the South considering itself subject to the North within the federation, carried out its frequent threat and desire of secession.

Dickens quotes Jefferson after the Louisiana Purchase, when there was talk of a division of the Union into an Atlantic federation and a Mississippi federation: "Let them part by all means if it is for their happiness to do so. It is but the elder and the younger son differing. God bless them both, and keep them in Union if it be for their good, but separate them if better." The breach was inevitable.

Though Dickens condemned slavery, he deemed it unlikely that it had been the cause of the war.

He asked: "If it be not slavery, where lies the partition of the interests that has led at last to actual separation of the Southern from the Northern States?" And the answer: In the original Constitution, wrote Dickens, it was provided that all taxes "shall be uniform throughout the United States." There it was again—tax uniformity.

In the beginning there were few manufacturers in the new nation. Import duties fell evenly among the states. But manufacturing got started after the War of 1812, and a modest protective tariff for the infant industries seemed to be in everyone's interest. By 1828, the protective tariff had become a prohibitive tariff, providing fat profits to manufacturing interests in the North—interests that no longer really needed protection. The tariffs turned into "a system that compelled it [the South] to pay a heavy fine into the pockets of Northern manufacturers." Southern ships that carried cotton and tobacco to Europe were paid by an "exchange of commodities," i.e., European manufactured goods, which now had a high tariff charge, thus draining money from southern pockets and depositing it in the federal Treasury. Northerners were not paying this tariff, yet they were benefiting from it. It was a tax that lacked uniformity, was unequal, and thus unconstitutional.

The South's last grievance, wrote Dickens, was the Morrill Tariff, which was a primary plank in the Republican platform in 1860. Immediately after the Congress met in March 1861, this highest of all tariffs was passed, with duties above 50 percent on iron products. This was an outrage to southerners. Even British and other European traders condemned it.

The South had loathed the tariff for nearly forty years, since it had made the price of cotton and tobacco decline. As they could not receive British or French goods in exchange with a high tariff, southern planters would have to demand hard cash, which in turn would require a lower price for their commodities. Dickens explained the South's predicament:

> Every year, as 1861 drew nearer, southern states had declared that they would submit to this extortion only while they had not the strength to resist. But with the election of Lincoln, and the growth of an exclusive northern party in the federal government, the time to resist had arrived.

So, reasoned Dickens,

> the case stands, and under all the passion of the parties and the cries of battle lie the two chief moving causes of the struggle. Union means so many millions a year lost to the South; secession means the loss of the same millions to the North. The love of money is the root of this as of many many other evils.

He ends with these words: "the quarrel between North and South is, as it stands, solely a fiscal quarrel."

John Stuart Mill—in Rebuttal

Within two months after Dickens' two articles on the cause of the American Civil War, John Stuart Mill published an article in the popular *Fraser's* magazine, in London. Mill popularized the view that slavery was the "one cause" of the conflict, and his February 1862 article attacked Dickens's logic with a vengeance. The article was soon reprinted in *Harper's* magazine in America. That theory, that slavery was the cause, has dominated Civil War thinking ever since.

1. Mill starts by charging that secession was for one purpose only, to extend and protect slavery. The renewed trading in slaves, said Mill, would lead to an Anglo-Confederate war. Great Britain would have to do what the North failed to do—destroy slavery in America. British warships would have to patrol the African coast to block slave-trading ships under Confederate control. This confrontation would lead to a war between the Confederacy and Great Britain.

The problem with Mill's opening argument is that he had not done his homework. The Confederate Constitution had been around for almost a year, and it clearly prohibited any slave trade by any of the southern states, "and Congress [Confederate] is required to pass such laws as shall effectively prevent the same." (Article I, Section 9)

2. Mill's next point focuses on slavery again. He notes that throughout Britain it is a common belief that "The North, it seems, have no more objection to Slavery than the South have. . . . They are ready to give it new guarantees; to renounce all that they have been contending for; to win back, if opportunity offers, the South to the Union by surrendering the whole point." Now, that is a fairly accurate statement of fact. But Mill sweeps it aside by insisting that the southern states are "fighting for slavery alone." The South "separated on slavery, and proclaimed slavery as the one cause of the separation."

3. The tariff, said Mill, was not the motive for secession because after the election of Lincoln in November 1860, the tariff then in effect was not too high. Moreover, the ultra-high protective tariff, the Morrill Tariff, did not exist until early March 1861. Mill ignored the apparent fact that a high tariff was both the Republican

Party's and most northerners' primary objective, regardless of their political affiliations.

A month before the election, on October 11,1860, the most outspoken and prominent southern newspaper, the *Charleston Mercury,* commented on the election of a Republican administration, charging that it would "plunder the South for the benefit of the North, by a new protective tariff."

Two days before the election in November, the *Charleston Mercury* continued its assault on the prospects of a Republican administration:

> The real causes of dissatisfaction in the South with the North, are in the unjust taxation and expenditure of the taxes by the Government of the United States, and in the revolution the North has effected in this government, from a confederated republic, to a national sectional despotism.

Five days before Louisiana withdrew from the Union, on January 21, 1861, the *New Orleans Daily Crescent* published this remarkable editorial, explaining the causes of secession:

> They [the South] know that it is their import trade that draws from the people's pockets sixty or seventy millions of dollars per annum, in the shape of duties, to be expended mainly in the North, and in the protection and encouragement of Northern interests. . . .
>
> These are the reasons why these people do not wish the South to secede from the Union. They [the North] are enraged at the prospect of being despoiled of the rich feast upon which they have so long fed and fattened, and which they were just getting ready to enjoy with still greater *gout* and gusto. They are as mad as hornets because the prize slips them just as they are ready to grasp it.

The South had been fighting for low, free trade–type tariffs since 1820. A recession in 1858 was blamed by northern manufacturers on the low tariff, and there was strong support for a high tariff throughout much of the North. The new tariff went through the Congress so fast that it was signed into law by President James Buchanan before Lincoln took the oath of office. With most southerners having left Congress, it was passed with little opposition from the floor.

If Mill had read almost any southern newspaper during the year prior to his article's publication in *Fraser's* magazine, he would never have written that the South was solely concerned with protecting slavery. Instead, he would have seen that a Republican victory would have meant the end of the South as an equal in the Union. Northern politics would have controlled the federal government and would have put the South in economic jeopardy.

4. The right of secession, said Mill, may be laudable. But with the South, it would be an enormous crime. The South has no real grievance—no right to revolt against the North. And since they are rebelling to protect and expand the institution of slavery, they have no more right to secede than would a band of robbers and criminals. He then compares the Confederate states to a couple of bands of famous highwaymen and robbers who had plundered the English countryside and were later captured and hanged. "The only real difference is that the present rebels are more powerful than Cartouche or Turpin [the notorious robbers and murderers], and may possibly be able to effect their iniquitous purpose." He likens the Confederates to a hypothetical situation in which a band of inmates at Parkhurst Prison on the Isle of Wight had seized the prison and taken over the island. Should the British government recognize a chain gang that had declared itself independent? Of course not, and that is the essence of what is happening in America.

Mill ends with full justification for the war and the northern invasion of the South. It was war for a good cause, a war of principle. By destroying slavery, the North would elevate its war on the "scale of morality and dignity . . . and the sense of an inestimable benefit to all future ages, brought about by their own voluntary efforts."

So the debate ended. Dickens did not directly respond.

Dickens was outraged at Mill for ignoring the cruel poverty of children and the homeless in London right under his nose while taking up the cause of unfortunates in faraway places Mill had never seen. Dickens saw the suffering of London's homeless children to be far worse than the plight of the children of North American slaves, whom he had seen in Richmond. As with Mr. Scrooge, he saw money as the root of most evils, including the War Between the States, centered on northern tax policies. The above is an original illustration entitled "Houseless and Hungry" from Dickens' novel Edwin Drood.

IT HELPS TO understand this fascinating contest in London between these two remarkable men of letters; it helps to learn of the contestants and their private lives. Dickens grew up in the slums and squalor of London. He was twelve years old when he was forced to abandon any formal education. Growing up in these conditions colored his view of life and found expression in his novels. He saw the horrors of poverty, the love of money and its evil as a force in society, government, and all levels of life. He saw the Civil War through this lens. He condemned John Stuart Mill, and those like him, for not taking notice of the social evils at home, and dwelling on apparent injustices across the oceans that were too often misunderstood.

Charles Dickens traveled to America and visited many of the states before the Civil War. He was not impressed. He believed slavery was an abomination. Politically, he thought the U.S. presidency was flawed. It produced corruption and mediocrity that were impossible to root out during the four-year tenure of each president. The system fostered misuse except when the president

This drawing depicts a planter announcing to West Indian slaves the emancipation of all slaves by Parliament in 1834. Dickens believed that the emancipation in America should come the same way, from the southern people, and not by force from the outside.

was an unusually great man, and the system didn't produce great men anymore. The Jeffersons, Madisons, and Monroes had been replaced with Tylers, Pierces, and Buchanans.

Though John Stuart Mill grew up in the same country and city as Dickens, no two men could have been more different in their upbringing. His father decided to raise his son in a cloistered environment, removed from the real world. He learned Greek, Latin, and a host of languages at an age not much beyond today's grammar school. He was to be a kind of superintellectual, to rise above all the learned of his day. In the end, a brilliant mind was produced, and Mill had a commanding position and respect in his day as a thinker. His analysis of the Civil War and slavery as its "one cause" found favor among northern apologists who wanted a simple answer to a national tragedy.

It was easy for northern apologists to agree with Mill. The southerners who tried to withdraw from the Union were vile criminals for trying to do so. Lincoln and his war party agreed with Mill on this score. The southerners were traitors, and ought to have been thankful for anything they received short of a hanging.

Dickens saw money as the root of the War Between the States. Unfortunately for the cause of history, it was Mill's, not Dickens', argument that was reproduced in the northern press, which was hungry for an excuse to invade the South. Mill's argument that slavery was the one cause of the Civil War became common wisdom, and the Dickensian view virtually disappeared, even among Ivy League Civil War historians who, like Mill, live in an economic cloistered world, which minimizes the role money plays in the affairs of men.

10

Taxes or War!

Lincoln has become one of the national deities, and a realistic examination of him is thus no longer possible.

—H. L. Mencken, 1931

In 1860 at Chicago, the Republican Party nominated Lincoln for the presidency. They also made clear what they intended to do if elected. One of the major planks in their platform was a high protective tariff. When it was introduced, the delegates yelled uproariously and threw their canes and hats in the air so suddenly it was "as if a herd of Buffalo had stampeded through the convention hall." The news spread quickly in the southern states. It became clear to southerners that a Republican administration would result in another "Tariff of Abomination." That fact, coupled with the Republican opposition to slavery, produced enough ire for most southerners to want out of the Union.

Prior to the Republican victory in 1860, there was a partnership in the federal government. The political parties were well-respected and supported in both North and South. There was no party hostile to southern interests. Now that had changed. For the "solid South," it was natural to want independence and to go their own way. The North was in control of the nation; they had the presidency, and they would soon have the votes in both houses of Congress. It would only be a short while before they had the Supreme Court, which at that time had a 5 to 4 majority in favor of the South; but the next vacancy on the Court would end that as well. It was time for the South to get out while the getting was good. No doubt, they could see the writing on the wall.

The dominant mood in the North was to compromise and save the Union. There was a flurry of activity to work something out, even after the solid South had left the Union, and its senators and representatives had gone home. Most other southerners in the administration, even in the army and navy, resigned and went home. Secession was a fact. But those who wanted desperately to preserve the Union, "as it was," tried hard. They offered the South a number of proposed constitutional amendments that would protect slavery, even in the territories. Lincoln himself, in his Inaugural Address, approved a new constitutional amendment (ironically number thirteen), which the Congress had just passed. It would protect slavery, and it could not be repealed. Some proposals went much further, but they were defeated, in part because the fire-eating southerners voted against them. That may seem strange, but the most die-hard southerners didn't want to be in the Union, no matter what was offered. They saw an independent South as a much more desirable political arrangement than a Union, even if the North was to give slavery more protection than it had ever before enjoyed.

Why did Lincoln take such a hard stand against secession? And why did he refuse to have any discussions with southern representatives who came to Washington to try to work out a peaceful settlement between the northern federation and the southern

Lincoln's Inaugural. Tom Nast, a twenty-one-year-old illustrator, made this caricature as his first political drawing. In the North, Lincoln was a man of peace, offering a constitutional amendment protecting slavery; in the South, Lincoln was demanding taxes or war!

Confederacy? No doubt he opted for war, when he could have had peace. These are questions that hinge on the tax issue more than anything else. If the prosperity of the North was of primary importance—and the destiny of the American empire was not to be jeopardized—then his decision to precipitate a war and coerce the South back into the Union, as conquered enemies or misguided citizens, seemed to be fully justified from that point of view. From the standpoint of the slaughter and the destruction of civilized life, this war was an outrage to humanity. The adverse consequences have survived to this day. But that, of course, is retrospective wisdom. Who in 1861, North or South, would have thought the war would have been such a calamity? Lincoln certainly didn't. His first call for volunteers to put down the rebellion was for four months' service—just enough time to get badly mauled in the First Battle of Bull Run.

Most foreign writers and correspondents saw the Civil War for what started it, and it was not started over slavery. The emancipa-

Lincoln's Inaugural Address in 1861, when he gave the South the option of—Taxes or War!

tion of the slaves came later, as a war measure. One British quarterly journal summed up the war rather accurately for 1862:

> For the contest on the part of the North is now undisguisedly for empire. The question of Slavery is thrown to the winds. There is hardly any concession in its favor that the South could ask which the North would refuse, provided only that the seceding States would re-enter the Union. . . . Away with the pretence on the North to dignify its cause with the name of freedom to the slave!

Lincoln's Inaugural Address in early March 1861 was to appease the South on the slavery question; he never invoked the Republican stand against slavery in the territories. Some in the North thought it was conciliatory—a nice speech—but southerners saw it for what it was, an ultimatum of "taxes or war."

Lincoln spoke with affection for the South, as if they were brothers, members of a common family. Yet the question of civil war rested with the South, for he would take no military action, "no invasion" of the South, except to collect taxes and recover any federal property. The few bits of federal property were really insignificant and of no value to speak of, and the southern states had not only offered to pay for all federal properties but sent a delegation to Washington to work out and settle the matter by peaceful negotiations. Lincoln refused to discuss the matter. The tax issue was hopeless, and Lincoln knew no southerners would pay taxes to the North.

One didn't have to read between the lines to know that war was inevitable. The question of civil war did not rest with the South, but with Lincoln, when his promised invasion to collect taxes would occur. To make it clear that taxes were the issue, the first act of aggression against the South took place within a week after Fort Sumter. Lincoln ordered a naval blockade against all southern ports. Under the rules of international law, a blockade is an act of war.

11

What on Earth Is the
North Fighting For?

War and imperialism, so long the most admired
of human activities

Kenneth Clark, *Civilization,* 1969

In 1862, a "special correspondent" for *Macmillan's* magazine, a
British monthly, went to America to find out for its readers,
"What on earth is the North fighting for?" The use of the exple-
tive "on earth" indicates a sense of bewilderment on the part of
most Europeans. The correspondent did a thorough job of investigating the North's motives for the war. He talked with northerners
from all walks of life, in many states, and summarized the answers
given in these words:

> We do not claim to be carrying on a war of emancipation; we are not
> fighting for the blacks, but for the whites. . . . The object of the war is
> to preserve the Union.

Preserving the Union had little to do with legalistic constitu-

Harper's 1861 article on Winfield Scott, "Commander in Chief of the Armies of the United States, who, in 1861, was entrusted with the conduct of the military operations in defense of the Government, the Constitution, and the Laws, against a conspiracy of demagogues to overthrow them." In answer to the question by a British war correspondent—what was the North fighting for?—he replied, "England, sir, is a noble country; a country worth fighting for." The correspondent interpreted this to mean that like England, America was also worth fighting for, and that was what the war was about to northerners.

tional issues, which were debatable. "It was for clear matter-of-fact interests." But when this correspondent tried to pin down these so-called matter-of-fact interests, the answers could hardly justify the carnage and destruction that was taking place. There were no high moral ideals at stake. He visited with the aging, senior general of the North, Winfield Scott, hero of the Mexican War (1846–47). The general answered with a question—The British Empire was worth fighting for, wasn't it? implying that the American empire was also worth fighting for.

Taxes probably started the war. Notice I do not use the phrase "caused the war." Since entire books have been written about the so-called causes of the Civil War, it would be simplistic and wrong to say that taxes were the *only* cause. They were, however, at the heart and the helm of the dispute.

The South had anticipated the high Morrill Tariff some six months before the Republicans pushed it through Congress. And it was a high tariff indeed, as iron products were taxed at 50 percent and clothing at 25 percent. It was considered by the free trade–thinking British as a *"prohibition tariff."* The Morrill tariff was certainly an affront to the South and made any return to the Union almost impossible. For forty-five years the South had been combatting northern high-tariff tax philosophy, and even though reasonable compromises had been worked out, that didn't satisfy southern political thinking. No doubt, the inevitability of the high tariff with the Republican victory in November 1860 did much to prompt the secession movement from words to deeds. One southern writer, who assisted in firing the first shot on Fort Sumter, wrote on the eve of the war (1860): "The Northern States would not have attained half of their present greatness and wealth, which have been built upon the tribute exacted from the South." Shortly after the war (1866), in a book appropriately called *The Lost Cause,* we read: "In every measure that the ingenuity of avarice could devise the North exacted from the South a tribute, which it could only pay at the expense and in the character of an inferiour in the Union."

The war started, not because of the high Morrill Tariff, but just the opposite: it was the low southern tariff, which created a free trade zone. That tariff and its economic consequences for the North—disastrous consequences—were what aroused the anger of northern commercial interests and turned their apathy toward the seceding states into militant anger. It united the money interests in the North, and they were willing to back the president with the capital needed to carry on the war. Here is the scenario:

1. On March 11. 1861, the Confederate Constitution was adopted. It created what was essentially a free trade zone in the Confederacy, in contrast to the new high-tax, protective zone in the North.

2. Within less than two weeks, northern newspapers grasped the significance of this and switched from a moderate, conciliatory policy to a militant demand for immediate action. Here are examples of three newspaper editorials, out of many, that gave Lincoln the backing he absolutely needed to take coercive action against the Confederates:

On March 18, 1861, the *Philadelphia Press* demanded war: "Blockade Southern Ports," said the *Press.* If not, a series of customshouses will be required on a vast inland border from the Atlantic to West Texas. Worse still, with no protective tariff, European goods will underprice northern goods in southern markets. Cotton from northern mills will be charged an export tax. This will cripple the clothing industry and make British mills and manufacturers prosper. Finally, the great inland waterways, the Mississippi and Missouri Rivers, and the Ohio River, will all be subject to southern tolls.

Previously, on January 15, 1861, the *Press* had been against any military action, arguing that it should be the policy of the northern government to settle its differences with the South peacefully, and not by conquest, subjugation, coercion, or war. The *New York Times* also changed its tune. For months their leading economic editor had been writing that secession was no threat to northern prosperity and commerce, and inaction was the best course for the government. But on March 22 and 23, 1861, he reversed himself with a demand that the federal government "At once shut up every Southern port, destroy its commerce, and bring utter ruin on the Confederate states. . . . A state of war would almost be preferable" to the passive action the government had been following.

Newspapers all over the country panicked over the thought of a southern free trade zone, and there is no doubt this fear was well justified. New York importers found their trade contracts canceled from Europe and rebooked to New Orleans. Baltimore was approached by the Confederacy and was offered complete tax freedom if it would join the Confederacy. There is no doubt that the Confederates were going to do to the Yankees what the Yankees had been doing to the South for over forty years—the Yankees would squirm now. The tax policy that had injured the South would reverse and southern tax policy would now cripple the North. Isn't turnabout fair play?

The best article on the South's free trade policy also came out on March 18, 1861, in the *Boston Transcript*. This insightful editorial spells out the southern game plan in no-nonsense language:

> It does not require extraordinary sagacity to perceive that trade is perhaps the controlling motive operating to prevent the return of the seceding states to the Union which they have abandoned. Alleged grievances in regard to slavery were originally the causes for the separation of the cotton states; but the mask has been thrown off and it is apparent that the people of the principal seceding states are now for commercial independence. They *dream* that the centres of traffic can be changed from Northern to Southern ports. The merchants of New Orleans, Charleston and Savannah are possessed with the idea that New York, Boston, and Philadelphia may be shorn, in the future, of their mercantile greatness, by a revenue system verging on free trade. If the Southern Confederation is allowed to carry out a policy by which only a nominal duty is laid upon imports, no doubt the business of the chief Northern cities will be seriously injured thereby.
>
> The difference is so great between the tariff of the Union and that of the Confederate States that the entire Northwest must find it to their advantage to purchase their imported goods at New Orleans rather than New York. In addition to this, the manufacturing interests of the country will suffer from the increased importation resulting

from low duties. . . . The [government] would be false to its obligations if this state of things were not provided against.

Less than two weeks after the newspapers in the North caught the militant fever for war, Lincoln called his cabinet on March 29, 1861, and asked for their views on sending a naval force to reinforce Fort Sumter, South Carolina. The leading members—secretaries of war, navy, interior, and the Attorney General—were certain it would start a war. The powerful secretary of state, W. H. Seward, had a problem. He had been telling the southern commissioners that Sumter would be abandoned shortly.

After the meeting, Lincoln surprised his secretaries of the navy and war with written instructions to proceed at once to prepare a naval task force to reinforce Fort Sumter. These instructions had been written the day before by an ex-navy captain who had been acting under Lincoln and bypassing the top brass. Lincoln then notified the governor of South Carolina that the task force would be coming with provisions "only" for the fort.

The garrison at Sumter had been receiving fresh food and meats daily from the markets in Charleston. They even had their own butcher. When they were out of cigars and other luxuries, these were also promptly provided. Later, the "starving garrison" scenario was used to justify the reinforcement. The southerners knew that "provisioning only" was not true, and that the main thing the garrison lacked was military provisions and soldiers, exactly what was on board Lincoln's task force. The South Carolinians knew from a few months before that the "provisioning only" was a fraud. In January 1861, President Buchanan had sent a single ship, the *Star of the West*, with troops and munitions hidden below deck. Unfortunately, the deception didn't work; southerners fired a volley of cannon balls across the bow of the ship, and it quickly turned and fled. When Lincoln's task force was on its way with troops, cannon, and military supplies, the Confederates knew better.

A scholar from Yale, writing in the *New Englander* during the

DEATH TO TRAITORS! This New York cartoon shows the nation's symbol, Columbia, with sword in hand after having slain a secessionist. On the blade are the words, UNION AND LIBERTY with the title, "Let it be ever thus with traitors."

war, pointed out that it was the objective of the Confederacy, with its secession and free trade, to bring "utter financial ruin on the North"—

> Northern industry was to be paralyzed; Northern looms were to be stopped; Northern merchants and banks were to suspend payment. The crowd of greedy Northern parasites, which had long fattened upon Southern wealth, were to be ejected forever from their posts and deprived of their ill-gotten gains. Universal bankruptcy and general impoverishment would break up the foundations of social order. Anarchy would reign in Northern cities, and grass would grow in their streets. (vol. XXII, p. 54)

If this was the objective of secession, and many northern propagandists proclaimed the same view, then it would not be too difficult to unite the North for war, invade the South, and destroy this dangerous enemy. In short, the northern aggression was really a preventive war—to prevent the destruction of the North by southern economic policy.

To arouse the northern populace for war, it was easy to make a preventive war out of "preserving the Union." It was another easy step to brand southerners as the aggressors, and thus as traitors.

Behind Lincoln's decision to provoke the South and start a war was the realization that the South's low-tariff zone would wreck northern business, manufacturing, and commerce. Herein lies the commercial justification for "preserving the Union." Not very noble, to be sure, but simple, basic hardnose economics, what most wars have in common. As for Sumter, it controlled the harbor at Charleston. Its guns might have been able to prevent any ship from entering or leaving the harbor, and Sumter was the chief Atlantic port of entry for the South. Maintaining that fort with adequate cannon and troops could have tied up southern commerce and crippled a major commercial center.

Lincoln's cabinet officers pointed out to Lincoln that the fort had no value now with secession, and it wasn't worth starting a war over a useless fort. But Lincoln saw it differently: Sumter was a prize to be maintained, and it could cripple and shut down the major Atlantic port of entry to the Confederacy. Rather than being of no value, as the secretaries maintained, it was in Lincoln's mind of value beyond measure. Lincoln often referred to poker and playing one's cards well, as he analyzed and developed his war policies. With Sumter, he played his cards exceedingly well. Either way, he was a winner.

He never explained this to his cabinet officers when he dismissed them on March 29, 1861. They were as surprised as the South was when they learned he was reinforcing Fort Sumter. But this was Lincoln's way. As his law partner later noted, "He was the most secretively—reticent—shut-mouthed man that ever lived."

Shortly after Lincoln's orders were given to reinforce Fort

Sumter, he was visited by a special envoy sent from Virginia, Colonel John B. Baldwin, who hoped to persuade Lincoln not to start a war over Sumter. Lincoln asked, what am I to do about those men in Montgomery? Colonel Baldwin urged him to wait until they could be peacefully brought back into the Union. Lincoln's reply is the main clue we have to his decision to reinforce Fort Sumter. Said Lincoln, "And open Charleston, etc., as ports of entry with their ten percent tariff. *What, then would become of my tariff?*" Baldwin later noted that "This last question he announced with such emphasis, as showed that in his view it decided the whole matter." Lincoln indicated to Baldwin that the interview was at an end, and dismissed him. A few days before, Lincoln had said almost the identical words to his cabinet officers.

At the time this meeting between Lincoln and Baldwin was going on, the naval squadron was being assembled on the high seas, to carry out plans to reinforce Fort Sumter. The game plan was to send 11 warships with a total of 2,500 men and 285 cannon for the so-called starving garrison. Starvation my foot! Behind the Sumter drama there loomed the issue of taxes, not food for 80+ soldiers, but revenue for Northern coffers.

The American Revolution was started over taxes; it is not surprising that the Second American Revolution was also started over taxes. Civil War buffs can argue over the causes of the war, but when you get down to the nuts and bolts of the conflict, it was initially over economics—a trade war.

The patriotic tax cartoon (page 109) shows a confident Uncle Sam sending naval expeditions against the South, financed with a high tariff and a bundle of internal taxes on just about everything— sales, manufacturing, income, real estate, stamps on documents, and transportation tickets. These early blockading operations crippled the South's hopes of establishing open and prosperous tax-free ports at the expense of Boston, New York, and Philadelphia.

This caricature is of special significance because it brought home to the people in the North the necessity for "tax, tax, tariff" to fi-

UNCLE SAM RAISING THE WIND TO A GOOD TUNE.
Uncle Sam (sings)—"Away! Away! Away down South in Dixie land—away!" etc.

A 1862 northern cartoon shows Uncle Sam singing, "Away! Away! Away down South in Dixie land, Away! etc.," with the title, "UNCLE SAM RAISING THE WIND TO A GOOD TUNE."

nance the war against the South. When Peter the Great of Russia organized a Senate to raise taxes for his wars to build a modern Russia, he told the senators, "Money is the heart of war, do ye gather in all that ye may." The Lincoln administration learned that lesson well. What is most amazing is that they were able to bring in such a large tax harvest without provoking a rebellion. Here's the reason why.

It has been difficult for many Civil War students to fathom why the northern states would sacrifice so much money and blood to conquer the South and force them to remain in the federal Union. It seems especially strange for a people who believed in government by consent to want to force on another people a government against their consent. And force they used, of monstrous proportions that shocked the civilized world. This was no minor military encounter. To take away from the southern people their right of self-determination, there had to be a massive destruction of life, of cities, of towns and villages, of farms and private homes—almost a total annihilation of the social order. Europeans looked upon this aghast, and reasoned that the Americans must have learned this kind of warfare from the native Indians, certainly not from their

European roots. Napoleon was a kindly gentleman compared to Grant, Sherman, and Sheridan.

A humorist writer, Tim Shay Arthur, was a forceful apologist for the North, especially for the income tax. He was noted for his little stories that prodded his countrymen into doing good. He promoted the temperance cause with his famous short story "Ten Nights in a Barroom." For the income tax, he came up with a fictional dialogue between two neighbors. It was called "Growler's Income Tax" (1864), and it sought to shame his compatriots into supporting the tax.

What makes this short story of great value is his portrayal of the reasons for the war—what the war was really about and why it deserves your money. The truism that the first casualty of war is truth may have got started with the Civil War and what the northern apologists tried to pass on to the people.

> My neighbor Growler [sounds like a true taxpayer], an excitable man by the way, is particularly excited over his income tax, or, as he called it, his "War Tax." He never liked the war—thought it unnecessary and wicked; the work of politicians. The fighting of brother against brother was a terrible thing in his eyes. If you asked him who begun the war?—who struck at the nation's life?—if self defense were not a duty?—he would reply with vague generalities, made up of partisan tricky sentences, which he had learned without comprehending their just significance.

The neighbor then tries to tell Growler he got the war all wrong. What would defeat mean? What if the rebellion had succeeded? "Have you ever pondered the future of this country in such an event?" the neighbor is asked.

A defeated America would be ripe for takeover by the English and French, Growler is told. Destruction from the South's "patricidal hands" would be too horrible to imagine. Southern armies "would have swept in desolation over the whole land. Traitors in our midst and traitors in arms against us would have united to destroy our beautiful fabric of civil liberty . . . who can tell under what iron rule we might have fallen. . . . But the wave of destruction was met—nay hurled back upon the enemies who sought our ruin." The neighbor then turns to Growler:

> And what does the nation assess you as your share of the costs of this security? Half your property? No, Not a farthing of that property! Only a small percentage of your income from that property! Pardon me for saying it, friend Growler, but I am more than half ashamed of you.

The old adage, "What Peter says about Paul tells you more about Peter than Paul," seems to have a place in the propaganda of the North to its people. They had turned the facts around—it was now the South that was seeking to subjugate and conquer the North, destroy her liberty, and wreak havoc upon the entire northern states. Under these circumstances, paying taxes was a small price to prevent a southern conquest. Thus "preserving the Union" came to mean saving the Union from destruction by Confederate armies and the South's free trade zone. It was not the destruction of the federal Union that was at issue, but the lives, property, and liberty of all the people.

If northerners bought this version of events, and they did, then it is no wonder they put up such a fight and sacrificed so much, for in their view, the end of civilization was at hand. Lincoln's Gettysburg Address was not mere poetry—the very survival of the North was at stake. If the South had won her independence, in Lincoln's immortal words, democratic government, government of the people, would have "perished from the earth."

AMERICA WAS FOUNDED by rebels, mostly tax rebels, who fled from Europe to escape harsh taxation. When the British tried to keep them subservient to the mother country, they used taxation as a symbol of the crown's authority over the colonists. The southerners saw their struggle in the same light.

The southerners in 1861 were also tax rebels, and in their writings and speeches they almost always made reference to their forebears who fought the British in 1776. By contrast, Lincoln became immortal in the North for his words referring to the founding of the nation upon the principle that "all men are created equal." The southern rebels saw the Declaration of Independence differently, as dedicated to the proposition that all governments "derive their just powers from the consent of the governed." Lincoln ignored that in his Gettysburg Address and in his policy toward the South. Most important, Lincoln did not believe in the right of the self-determination of peoples. Most Americans are unaware of that unavoidable but unpleasant conclusion. Preserving the Union, the American empire, came first and foremost, above all else.

Why is it that the southern people have not given up their rebel past, still holding fast to the Confederate battle flag flying atop state buildings, and even incorporating it into the official state flags? As an unknown author said,

> You can fight and beat revolutions as you can fight and beat nations. You can kill a man, but you can't kill a rebel. For the proper rebel has an ideal of living, while your ideal is to kill him so that you may preserve yourself. And the reason why no revolution has ever been beaten is that rebels die for something worth dying for, the future, but their enemies only die to preserve the past, and the makers of history are always stronger than the makers of empires.
>
> —*The American Historical Review,* XXXI, July 1926

IV

THE TYRANNY OF
THE REVENUERS

1865–1900

Federal agents from the Internal Revenue Bureau successfully assault and arrest moonshiners. One lies dead on the ground, while armed Treasury agents arrest those not killed. The right to kill anybody who offends federal regulations is still with us, as Waco, Texas, and Ruby Ridge, Idaho, bear sad witness.

Moonshiners have been traditional heroes, representatives of a stubborn individualism that appeals to Americans' resentment of government interference in their lives. Moonshiners have also been presented as simple country folk, victims of outside forces beyond their understanding or control.

—Wilbur R. Miller *Revenuers and Moonshiners* (1991)

Federal taxmen who were to literally invade the South and assault southern moonshiners were not the first federal taxmen to plunder the defeated Confederate states. Even before the whiskey tax revenuers appeared, the Treasury Department sent federal taxmen to the South to collect a land tax Congress had enacted soon after the Civil War started. How could this be, when the southern states were not part of the Union at that time? The Civil War was only an internal rebellion, and so the tax was still due and payable from each of the states. Whether the Civil War was a war between foreign governments or an internal revolt depended on what best suited Washington. After Lincoln's death, a malicious group of radicals controlled Congress, and they were determined to strip the South of its wealth—whatever was left after the war's devastation. Any rationale to steal everything in sight was the order of the day. Taxes were the best way to do that.

The direct land tax of 1861 carried a new penalty of 50 percent for delinquency, not unlike our tax penalties today. Special federal tax commissioners were empowered to collect the land tax, and they were empowered to sell any land that did not pay the tax.

Most of the proceeds from the tax never made it to Washington, but were simply stolen by corrupt tax collectors. The system was so bad that the secretary of the Treasury, Hugh McCullock, commented, "I am sure I sent *some* honest men south, but it sometimes seems doubtful whether any of them remained honest very long."

The land tax was a one-shot deal, so the punitive radicals enacted an excise tax on all cotton—the main crop of the South. Surely this would punish the South; this would be a burdensome, punitive tax, a kind of tribute to repay the North for the costs of the war. The tax was repealed, however, in 1868, shortly after it was put in force. The radicals in Congress had not thought the tax through. Most cotton was exported, and the primary importers were the mills and manufacturers in the North. A tax is an expense, and it was simply added to the cost of the cotton and passed on to northern manufacturers, increasing the cost of northern manufactured products. It didn't take long for northern commercial interests to force Congress to repeal the tax.

Even this excise tax was a failure, as the new breed of corrupt federal tax collectors stole this tax money as well. Records show that not even the federal Treasury benefited very much. But the new excise on whiskey, enacted as a war tax, continued. Except for this whiskey tax, only the tariff continued as a mainstay for revenue collection, and it remained ultra-high.

With the high tariff enforced upon the South after the war, the South once again bore a disproportionate tax burden when its economy started running again. To add to the outrage, this high tariff was used to finance the large pensions and benefits paid to the veterans of the Grand Army of the Republic, but not one penny was ever paid for pensions, disabilities, or the illnesses of the Confederate veterans. The bitter tax pill that helped spark the southern rebellion continued.

Unlike the First Whiskey Rebellion during Washington's time, which lasted only a few months, this Second Whiskey Rebellion of the moonshiners lasted for decades. Even to this day, "white lightning" is still a southern delight.

12

Discovering the Roots of the IRS and The Second Whiskey Rebellion

> You are hereby notified that 15 days will be al-
> lowed you to wind up your affairs & leave this
> county for good, if you do not take heed, you
> must abide the consequences.
>
> —Letter to a South Carolina revenue officer from
> the KKK

At the same time the above letter from the Ku Klux Klan was received, a deputy marshal in the same county also received a threatening letter: "Theas few lines is to let you know that you must leave . . . by 10 o Clock to Morrow or the Kucluck will kill ever one of you." "Kuclux" means being bushwhacked.

The notorious Ku Klux Klan has in our time been given an in-famous label for its cruelty toward southern blacks and for its white supremacy stand. Initially, the Klan was formed in Tennessee by disenfranchised veterans of the Confederacy. The Radical Republicans after Lincoln's death destroyed the political rights and power of the southern establishment and brought in carpetbaggers—

northern Yankee federal bureaucrats and with the votes of ex-slaves—to take over southern governments and rule southern society. In all ages any such activities, often by conquering armies, have led to underground, secret societies. They existed in ancient Israel under Roman despotism. During the American Revolution there were the Sons of Liberty. They would exist later in Russia throughout the Tsarist and Communist dictatorships.

In the early days of the Klan, the main targets were federal revenue officers, deputy marshals, informers, and especially black informers. The Klan thus became the underground organization for moonshiners fighting the federal tax collector and the alien federal bureaucrats who invaded from the North to reconstruct the society of the Confederacy. Some writers have made the distinction between the good Klan of the post–Civil War period and the bad Klan of the twentieth century. We can sympathize with the earlier Klan, which eventually would dominate all state governments after the carpetbaggers left in 1878. Time and again southern state governments sent complaints to Washington about the abuses and misconduct of federal tax agents of the Internal Revenue Bureau. Then, as now, the complaints fell on deaf ears. Thus the rebellion against federal tax laws was both above the ground and underground.

The North Carolina legislature sent a complaint to the Congress charging that the federal tax law was "oppressive and inquisitorial . . . legalizing unequal, expensive, and iniquitous taxation, and as enforced in this state, is a fraud upon the sacred rights of our people, and subversive of honest government." Alabama's legislature made a similar complaint, that federal taxmen had "raided over our country with large bodies of armed men and, regardless of law and decency, have abused and insulted the people without cause." Georgia complained that the heavy-handed federal taxmen were engaged in a policy "to terrify the people into obedience."

Of course the taxpayers fought back—the "moonshiners," as they were called—and this became the Second Whiskey Rebellion. It was not a peaceful rebellion. Instead of lasting a couple years, it lasted over thirty years. There were casualties on both sides, and murders on both sides—lots of them.

This tax rebellion, frequently looked upon as only a local struggle by what were often semiliterate, poor farmers, in the backwoods of Appalachia, was a major event in the history of the states in that region. It was even more significant in the history of the twentieth century, for in that rebellion the Internal Revenue Bureau (IRB) was born, and it started the expansion of federal power over all citizens for taxes, and soon spread from a simple tax on whiskey to regulation over all aspects of our civilized life.

The muscle of the old IRB, which developed in dealing with the moonshiners, has carried over into our century. The IRB was the forerunner of things to come; it set the stage and provided the spirit upon which all federal bureaucracies were to operate. Understand this early tax event, and you will understand your federal government today. It is just much bigger, but it is a carbon copy of that early bureaucratic extension of federal power.

This was a real rebellion, and not a peaceful one, either. The extent of the violence and viciousness on both sides would suggest that this was an extension of the Civil War, for the revolt started soon after Appomattox. Federal taxmen, with the support of local law enforcement and civilian posses, scoured the mountains for stills making untaxed whiskey. They destroyed thousands of stills over the decades that followed, killed scores of men, and arrested and sent to jail thousands more for evading a tax on whiskey ranging from 50¢ to $2 a gallon. The moonshiners were not all dyed-in-the-wool Confederates carrying on the Civil War. Many had evaded the fray; many were deserters, who looked upon the war as the rich man's war and wanted no part of it. There may have been as many Union sympathizers as Confederates. They had organized secret societies against the Confederacy, with a bewildering array of passwords, signs, grips, and blood-curdling oaths. They were against government—Confederate as well as Union. The support

Fighting for "the right to make a little licker." From Samuel G. Blythe, "Raiding Moonshiners," Munsey's magazine, 25 (June 1901), pp. 418–24.

for the Union during the Civil War may have been more of a backlash against local Confederate power, especially with conscription in April 1862. When the Union moved in after the Civil War, the enemy changed.

The use of such excessive amounts of deadly force for what was simply tax evasion may seem outrageously uncivilized in our day, but that is not so. The lethal force used in Waco, Texas, against a religious cult for a similar type of federal infraction may be traced to the force used against moonshiners. It seems that in enforcing the whiskey tax, no amount of force against the evaders was thought excessive, and that same policy of the right to use deadly force in enforcing most federal laws seems to have carried over to our day.

Federal taxmen and their armed escorts didn't hesitate to shoot and kill moonshiners, even when they were simple farmers making corn liquor for their own use. These simple mountain people fought back and meted out violence in return. Even those who sold some of their corn liquor were often selling the only cash crop available to them. Rarely were they living above the poverty line. They argued that they had just as much right to grind their corn into mash for liquor as they did to grind their corn into meal for bread. Furthermore, moonshiners had a long tradition of making "a little licker." It was something their fathers had been doing for decades. Thus they were "soundly convinced that the law is unjust, and that they are only exercising their natural rights." So long as these mountain people did no harm to their neighbors, they considered making mountain dew a natural and inalienable right. A Georgia moonshiner told a government prosecutor, "He'd like to know what his grandfather 'fit' in the Revolution for if he was not to be allowed to make a little corn whiskey."

The opposition included all ranks of society, even those of Republican persuasion. A North Carolina federal judge, whom you might expect to be supportive of federal law, observed

> Prominent political speakers of both political parties often address the people and for the purpose of winning popular favor, denounced in strong language the *injustice wrong, oppression,* and *outrage* of the Internal Revenue Laws. These laws have but few defenders except the Courts and the officers of the Government.

Women were in the fray along with their men. One lady was charged with attempted murder for shooting at a revenue officer. The local judge, trying to provide her with a defense of lacking criminal intent, suggested that maybe she didn't really intend to kill the tax officer. She retorted, "Of course I tried to kill him. My only regret is that I missed!" Revenue agents complained about the vulgarity and profanity the women shouted at them as they passed through the countryside. Other women sounded all kinds of alarms to warn the moonshiners of the coming of the revenuers. But the strangest story involved a man who, for a ten-dollar reward, turned in one of his neighbors. He was subsequently bushwhacked and killed. Neither his mother nor his wife expressed any remorse.

The military, while called into the service of the tax authorities, was never very enthusiastic about this calling. General William T.

Sherman, of Civil War fame and infamy, did not like having his soldiers used for tax collection, and his lukewarm acceptance of orders from above may have resulted in very few military casualties. Even the moonshiners withdrew from more hostile action when federal troops were accompanying tax posses. The troops and their officers showed little desire to act as tax collectors.

Perhaps the reason was the lack of any inducement other than their regular pay. On the other hand, tax collectors and deputies received payment for the number of arrests made and warrants issued. This kind of "piecework" helped to corrupt the administration when it became apparent that a lot of innocent people were being arrested and put in jail on the flimsiest of evidence. Many judges refused to sign arrest warrants without an exceptional showing of just cause; others, in some localities, wouldn't sign them at all.

This "piecework" compensation was supposedly justified because otherwise no one would take the job. It was not only unpopular but extremely dangerous in many regions. Revenuers traveling around the countryside had difficulty obtaining food and lodging at any price. With many of the menfolk languishing in local jails, and others wounded and even killed, revenuers found little favor in most localities. At the same time, local law enforcement often came down hard on revenue men. In the period from 1876 to 1879, the IRB reported a total of 165 of its officers prosecuted in state courts. The bureau acknowledged that many of its officers were "the roughest sort of illiterate men, who were unnecessarily severe," and that "Prosecutions have been brought in some districts, apparently only for the purpose of making fees. Great injustice is thus done to individuals and the Government."

The worst scandal with the revenuers was the use of "professional witnesses." Often they were relatives of the taxmen, and they would travel from district to district to give testimony against innocent farmers. In the South, some efforts were made to prosecute these professional witnesses for perjury because of the great injustice they created. Unfortunately, this piecework approach, with payments for the number of arrests made as well as the payments to informers and witnesses, only aggravated the local populace and added some justification for their violence against trumped-up charges and corrupt tax administration.

Occasionally, the enforcement became humorous when moonshiners responded to an arrest warrant by bringing their families to act as witnesses so that they could receive the appropriate witness fee and travel allowance. The moonshiner was usually fined $100, but that was often waived with a "poverty oath." Jail, for many moonshiners, was a vacation with free meals. Many sheriffs would let the moonshiner roam around town, playing cards and drinking whiskey, provided he returned for "eatin' and sleepin'." In a couple of months he'd be back with his family. This, however, was not the rule.

One aspect of this tax rebellion that may be of special interest to legal students is the jockeying by the participants for favorable tribunals. Assaulting or killing a federal taxman was only a state offense. No federal law was violated. This meant that moonshiners and revenuers would both be tried in state and local courts; however, federal courts could also try these same state offenses. Thus we had federal taxmen trying to be tried in federal courts, and moonshiners opting for local courts. Lawyers had a field day trying to get their man before the most biased court possible. Even today, the selection of the best or most favorable tribunal is foremost in the mind of tax practitioners.

Federal law was limited to the tax issues. Evaders were not felons, but had only committed a misdemeanor. Yet this didn't deter the use of deadly force against them, which seems hardly excusable by civilized standards. Today we have overcome that complaint, as we make almost everything a felony, and after 1934, assaulting a federal taxman became a federal offense.

There were times when there may have been as many federal taxmen in local jails as there were moonshiners. So if a federal officer assaulted or killed a moonshiner, he could be prosecuted in local courts, with judges and juries not sympathetic to his demeanor or his cause. Federal courts could also try federal officers for violation of state laws, but getting a state court proceeding transferred to a federal court was often impossible when a local judge refused to make the transfer.

One notorious case of the time, which dragged on for four years, from 1878 to 1882, involved a federal officer named Durham in an incident in South Carolina. Durham, leading a posse in early June, set out to arrest a moonshiner, Lewis Redmond, who had led a raid on a county jail to release some fellow moonshiners. The posse surrounded what they thought was a house he was visiting. The revenuers charged the house, and when a man in the house started for the back door, Durham shot him twice in the back as he was fleeing, thinking he was the outlaw Redmond. He wasn't, and he died shortly thereafter.

The federal officers claimed they had a warrant (which they didn't), but to cover their misdeed, they backdated a warrant to try to justify their mistake. In the end, the case was transferred to the federal court and Durham was acquitted. Southern newspapers condemned the proceedings, and charged that most tax officers were "men utterly deprived in character . . . more in harmony with the blind and despotic governments of the East than with the institutions of a free and enlightened Republic."

The legislatures from the states where the moonshiners were operating frequently sent petitions and complaints to Congress and the national government protesting about the injustice of the whiskey tax and the outrageous administration. Nevertheless, even with many northerners opposed to rigorous enforcement in the Mountain states, the Internal Revenue Bureau won the struggle for a time, in spite of casualties, state harassment, and public anger over the intrusion into their lives. The deciding factor was the head of the bureau, a Civil War general named Green B. Raum. He was determined to enforce the tax law, whatever the costs, and by the

1880s, resistance against the tax law began to wane as numerous detachments of deputies and posses scoured the Appalachians making hundreds of arrests—often granting amnesty to those who would simply promise not to make any illegal liquor without paying the required tax.

Informers were an important third party to this whiskey rebellion. They were from four main groups: first, neighbors with a grudge against a particular moonshiner, like the very famous feuding between the Hatfields and the McCoys. Both families were making illegal whiskey until one of the McCoy clan turned in a Hatfield to claim a reward, and thereby started the feud. Second were those who operated commercial stills and paid their taxes. Obviously, the moonshiners could undersell the higher-priced taxed liquor. Third were those who were in it for the money—witness fees and rewards for informing. Finally, in the end, were the prohibitionists. The temperance movement was picking up steam about this time. They saw liquor as the Devil's work, and with religious and self-righteous motives they joined in the fray against the moonshiners. This became especially significant as many counties and even states became "dry."

The danger for informants was great, and many an informer was later ambushed and murdered by angry moonshiners. Considering the risks involved, it is a wonder that anyone undertook such an endeavor. The prohibitionists and revenuers didn't always get along. Their objectives were different, even antagonistic. The revenuers were after taxes, legal and illegal. They had jobs to defend, and if all whiskey was illegal and all distilling was prohibited, there would be no work for them and no pay. Many times, in dry areas, the local law enforcement received no cooperation from the federal taxmen. Their tax rolls were kept away from the prying eyes of local lawmen who wanted to shut down all liquor operations. To local lawmen, those who paid their honest whiskey taxes were just as criminal as those who didn't. To the revenuers, they were job security.

There are many lessons to be learned from the Second Whiskey

Tax Rebellion, some as old as history and still not learned. In 1894, to raise additional federal tax revenues without increasing the tariff, Congress did the obvious—increased the whiskey tax so as to increase tax revenues. Simple logic, which has been tried many times in history and which has done just the opposite too often, the present day being our best example.

The need for more revenue arose out of the financial Panic of 1893. The tax rate of an acceptable 50 cents per gallon was raised to a hefty $1.10, which should have doubled tax receipts. Instead, revenues declined dramatically—not because people stopped drinking whiskey, but because of tax evasion and a mushrooming of illicit stills not just in the Appalachians but throughout the entire nation.

This folly did not go unnoticed, any more than the tax increases later under Presidents Bush and Clinton. Politicians can't seem to get beyond the supposedly simple mathematics of tax increases. It seems irrefutable to them that if you double the tax rate, you will ipso facto double the tax revenues. And although taxpayers have never responded that way, governments keep hoping they will.

When this massive tax increase for whiskey was proposed, David A. Wells, an economist who developed the revenue laws during the Civil War, warned against the high tax rate. It would foster evasion, he said; and it surely did. The government expected more revenues, yet it got less. But the increased tax rates did keep the revenuers busy. Arrests almost doubled in one year, from 487 (1892–93) to 871 (1894–95). Seizures of illegal stills increased during these same periods from 1,016 to 2,273. It was tax revenues that plummeted to well below the 1892–93 levels. They did not recover until 1899. All in all, it was a simple lesson in human nature in the face of excessive taxation.

Our First Whiskey Rebellion, in 1794, brought dramatic change in the federal system. The Federalist Party disappeared from history as these taxes on whiskey also disappeared. The people wanted less federal government, not more, and Jefferson, as the great champion of less federal power, set the stage for the next sixty years of American political history. But with the coming of the Civil War, war powers multiplied beyond anything imaginable in a country where most sovereignty was to reside in the states. War powers are known to do that, and war taxes are also known to continue after war is over.

So when the Civil War ended, federal bureaucracy continued for over a decade, centered most of all in military rule over the South, called Reconstruction. But Reconstruction failed, and the federal government gave up its bureaucratic powers over the conquered South. The South would govern itself once again. What did remain, however, was federal taxing power over this region that was not there before the Civil War. Thus, while the carpetbaggers disappeared, and one federal agency after another withdrew from American society, the Internal Revenue Bureau stayed on and established itself as a permanent part of national life. The federal justice system and the federal tax bureau reached into the lives of the southern people and cemented themselves as a permanent institution.

The whiskey tax was hardly taxation by consent. Worse still were the brutal enforcement procedures that brought forth lethal force, if necessary, against an unwilling population. The tax system shifted from one supposedly based on consent to one based on fear and brutality, putting rebellious taxpayers on the same plane as villains: men who were otherwise excellent citizens, poor but proud and independent, except for an unjust tax. And most of all, they had a national tradition and a war for independence to excuse and justify what they did.

The spirit of the Internal Revenue Bureau lived on and its policy of armed aggression against the disobedient eventually infected new federal bureaucracies that were to intrude into the lives of most citizens. In time its powers to enforce all taxation, however bad, became a driving force as it took over income tax duties. Enforcing an income tax in the entire nation simply mirrored the enforcement of the whiskey tax in Appalachia.

The outcome of the Second Whiskey Rebellion was quite different from the first rebellion, which ended when Jefferson took office in 1800 and repealed the tax. The rebels won. But the second rebellion never did end, and is still with us without the violence. In a sense the moonshiners won, as the Internal Revenue Bureau found bigger fish to fry when the federal income tax was adopted. It made no economic sense to expend the Treasury's resources chasing after a remotely scattered bunch of country folk making a little "corn licker." Thousands of moonshiner stills were, and still are, hidden in the woods for a thousand miles, from North Carolina to Oklahoma, and from the Gulf to Kentucky. The exploits of today's moonshiners have found expression in many of the popular ballads of country music. Merle Haggard's famous "Okie from Muskogee" prefers "white lightning" to smoking marijuana, while flying "old glory down at the courthouse." George Jones's most popular ballad is "White Lightning" with a chorus that begins:

> G-Men, T-Men, Revenuers too,
> looking for the place
> where my pappy made his brew.

V

THE TYRANNY OF
THE INCOME TAX

1913–199?

— Drawing by Allan Bunce

The Tyranny of the Income Tax

As the nineteenth century came to a close, the tax principles of the founders began to disappear. The idea of limited government was replaced with the zeal for paternalism in government at home and imperialism abroad. Wolves began to appear in sheep's clothing. Words that once stood for the noblest ideals of Western society took on strange and alien meanings. The state could take away anyone's property through crushing taxation and this was "social justice," or "revenue sharing." The Communist states called themselves "democratic" republics, and, in the end, taxes, for some, were the government's word for stealing. Or as one famous Supreme Court justice, John Harlan, called it, legislative plunder under the guise of taxation. The income tax became the fuel for paternalism in government, just as excises and land and wealth taxes had done in Europe centuries before.

Rebellion against the income tax began with the very first peacetime tax law, even though the rate was a paltry 2 percent. But modern income tax rebellions have taken a different course from the tax rebellions of the past, which were punctuated by riots and violence. Our income tax rebellions are quiet rebellions, taking place on the political field, in the schemes of tax planners, in peaceful emigration abroad, in the underground economy, in the privacy of tax haven institutions, legal and not-so-legal.

Today, riot or violence over taxes is unthinkable. Riots usually come from the masses, and the income tax has been engineered to be oppressive primarily to the rich, unlike many taxes of the past that provoked rebellion because they were uniformly applied. An excise like Walpole's tax on tobacco and wine hit all Britishers, and successful riots followed. The stamp taxes in America, again, applied to everyone. But the income tax, because of exemptions and low rates for the lower classes, makes riots unlikely. Even when it was first instituted, the rich were the targets, and, like half-starved crows, they did not sit around to be shot at. Their wealth, as if by magic, began to disappear. Violence made no sense when an accountant or tax professional with a briefcase could engineer a very successful tax rebellion, with no blood, no mess, no yelling, no damage to private property or public tax offices, no assaults or lynchings of tax agents.

There is probably no tax in the past two hundred years that has been more debated, discussed, cussed, ridiculed, praised, and in the end, evaded, than the income tax. The British, who, as we shall see, invented the modern income tax, hated it so much that the generation of Britons who experienced the first income tax had to pass away before the British government would dare try to introduce it once again. When it was finally reintroduced in Britain, it came in such a mild form one could hardly believe it had been the reputed "tyranny" of the Napoleonic world. One of the last holdouts was France, and it took a world war for them to get on the income tax bandwagon. The United States also climbed aboard at that time.

In America, the debate raged hot and heavy. *Harper's* magazine was especially hard on the tax, depicting it as the arch enemy of liberty, and a demoralizing force in society. The income tax would become a millstone around the neck of Liberty, as the following cartoon shows:

This cartoon in 1878, entitled "Peace with a War Measure," accepts the income tax as a war tax, not fit for a peacetime society because of its destruction of liberty.

By the beginning of the twentieth century the income tax was on its way to becoming the engine for running the modern state, for financing wars, and introducing socialism in its many forms. This was not the kind of world the founders had envisioned, but each generation that comes to power introduces its own ways of governing. Now, as this century comes to a close, the income tax seems to have run its course, as all taxes usually do. We are once again searching for a better way to tax. Our income tax has evolved into a revenue system that threatens liberty at every turn, and no doubt, most of the problems are of our own making. One of the lessons of tax history that recurs so often is that all good tax systems tend to go bad, and our income tax is a shining example. The excise became anathema to the Netherlands and Spain, as did other taxes that have appeared on the world's scene, which blossomed for a century or two and then disappeared in violence, economic decline, or collapse.

The story of our income tax goes back to Great Britain, which invented this monster and then passed it on to the world. This, then, is where we begin our study—where the income tax was born.

> The harvest of the Exchequer [revenue authority] has been very considerable while the misery inflicted on hundreds of thousands of taxpayers, both innocent and guilty, is beyond description. It is very difficult for officials, even with the best will in the world, to administer an inquisitorial law with humanity.
>
> —James Coffield, *A Popular History of Taxation,* 1970

13

The Goose That Laid the Golden Egg

One day a farmer, going to the nest of his goose,
discovered a golden egg, and every morning to
his delight he found another egg of pure gold.
He soon became rich by selling his golden eggs.
As he grew rich he grew greedy; and thinking to
get at once all the gold the goose could give, he
killed it and opened it only to find—nothing.

—Aesop's *Fables*

While the income tax was indeed a goose that laid a golden
egg, similar geese have come and gone in history, each
equally productive of revenue. The reason these taxes have disappeared is the reason our income tax will probably disappear in the
next century. Governments inevitably kill the goose that lays the
golden egg. The income tax in the latter half of the nineteenth
century was a very good tax, for it replaced a myriad of burdensome and nonproductive taxes that British society was anxious to
jettison. Consider the following caricature of an overburdened

THE BRITISH LION.

The British Lion with a mountain of taxes on his back.

British Lion, with a mountain of taxes on his back, taxes on just about everything imaginable:

Governments have been taxing income in many ways as long as there have been civilized life and historical records. But the modern income tax is of recent vintage, invented by the British around 1800 to finance the wars with Napoleon. It was, by our standards, an extremely simple tax, but Britishers didn't see it that way, as this 1800 caricature on the following page shows.

The British soon developed an extreme hatred for the income tax. It was a marvelous invention for raising revenue, but the British people wanted it used only during wars. To them, it was tyranny in its worst form. So when Napoleon got tucked away off the coast of Africa where he could no longer endanger the peace of Europe, the tax was repealed. But this was not an ordinary repeal. The British people not only wanted the law abolished, they wanted all records of the law destroyed—burned tax records tell no tales. The leader of the opposition to the tax brought forth cheers

John Bull (the English people) studies his first income tax form (1800), with his guardian angel telling him, "Trust your Fortune's care to me." To himself he says, "I have read many crabbed things in the course of my time—but this for an easy piece of Business is the toughest to understand I ever met with." That tax form was "a piece of cake" compared to the insanity of our present tax forms.

from the House of Commons when he thundered, "This extension of bureaucratic power into everyday life might be the herald of an all embracing tyranny." As the records were burned, the chancellor of the exchequer actually stoked the fires while they were burning, secretly retaining a duplicate copy of the records in the basement of the tax court.

European cartoonists in the eighteenth and nineteenth centuries loved to depict taxes as a many-headed monster, and the first modern income tax was no exception. Britain's most renowned cartoonist, Cruikshank, marked the repeal of the income tax in 1816 with

A Battered Britannia.

the following cartoon. A battered Britannia on the ground is told, "Rise Britannia! A Monster that so long oppressed and trampled on you is at last Subdued." Members of Parliament wielding their clubs on the monster shout: "Down, Down to hell! & say I sent thee!!"

No doubt a great percentage of American taxpayers would like to send their Internal Revenue Code "Down to Hell, and say I sent thee!!"

With most of the Napoleonic generation gone by the 1840s, the crown cautiously brought forth another income tax, but not one like the earlier tax that was so hated. This time the tax was a flat 3 percent, withheld at the source. Even then, the prime minister, Sir Robert Peel, apologized for the tax; he said it would be for three years only, and the intrusions into the financial affairs of the citizens would be minimal. Although this new leadership had not experienced the earlier income tax, they had certainly heard about it from their predecessors. As a special inducement, the crown repealed a 150-year-old door-and-window tax, illustrated in a caricature of 1843:

PEEL'S BANE AND ANTIDOTE.

Sir Robert. (log) " Come, Johnny, be a good boy, take it like a Man, and I'll give you a bit of Sugar."

Sir Robert Peel's new brand of income tax replaced a 150-year-old window-and-door tax, which in its time had replaced a de-spised chimney tax. In this cartoon, Sir Robert Peel is pictured as a governess, popular in England at that time. Little "Johnny Bull" (the English people) is told: "Come, Johnny, be a good boy; take it like a man, and I'll give you a bit of sugar."

This very modest income tax greatly influenced American atti-tudes and taxmaking policies. The tax did not end after three years, as promised. It continued and continued, right up to the present day. Many of the prime ministers who took office after the 1840s said that they would end the tax—as our presidents say they will balance the budget—but none of them did. The reason? The in-come tax brought forth a great revenue harvest; it produced more money than ever anticipated, and thus the British government sim-ply could not let go of it.

The same tenacity manifested itself in America. The Civil War brought forth an income tax in both the North and the South,

This cartoon in the British periodical, Punch, *indicates why the income tax could not be abolished, even though British leaders hated the tax (so they said) but could not bring themselves to abolish it. It produced a £6 million surplus.*

with considerable hatred on both sides. A Democratic opponent of Lincoln in the 1864 election period condemned the income tax: "Through a tax law, the like of which has never been imposed upon any but a conquered people, they [the Republicans] have possession . . . of the entire property of the country."

Lincoln was so upset with the attack on his war policy and income tax that he had this Democratic candidate arrested and tried before a military court in Ohio for the trumped-up charge of expressing treasonable sentiments. Lincoln personally signed the order banishing him from the country, notwithstanding the advice of his Attorney General that Lincoln was depriving an innocent man of his constitutional rights (free speech). Today, that would have been a serious criminal offense under the Civil Rights Act and would have justified impeachment. But, of course, that was a different time.

The South was no better than the North, nor Jefferson Davis than Lincoln, so far as income taxes were concerned. One prominent confederate leader wrote some years after the war:

The Richmond government nevertheless grew speedily into despotism and for four years wielded absolute power over an obedient and uncomplaining people. It levied taxes of an extraordinary kind upon a people already impoverished almost to a point of starvation.

The "taxes of an extraordinary kind" were income taxes.

By the end of the Civil War, the income tax had expanded to the point where from 10 to 15 percent of all households were paying the tax. It had an exemption of $600 annually, and most of the taxes were collected at the source, i.e., withheld. Unlike the British war income tax of the Napoleonic times, the Union tax continued for seven years, with some rate reduction and increases in exemptions.

On September 7, 1865, a new weekly periodical was born. About the same size as our current *Time* magazine, it was called *The Nation,* and is still published today. In the very first edition, the editors praised the American people for their support of the income tax: "No fact speaks so well for the loyalty of the American people, and in support of their determination to pay their debts as the readiness with which they submit to the payment of war taxes in times of peace." By contrast, in Britain in 1816, the British people abolished their war income tax with an annihilation of the system, even though the war debt was a staggering £800 million. The British government had promised the people that the tax was for the duration of the war, "and no longer."

It was true that in the North no such promise was made, but it seemed taken for granted by the people that the tax would end with the war. The editors of *The Nation* concluded: "It is a tax that can be defended only by the necessity of the case, seeing that it bears hard upon men of moderate means, and that it is by its nature essentially inquisitorial."

Six years after the income tax was repealed, it was being reconsidered. *Harper's* magazine attacked the income tax with the caricature below.

The fear that income tax would destroy liberty began to disappear as the British experience with its 3 percent income tax proved otherwise. It became clear that an income tax, if modest in all respects—in its tax rates, surveillance, equality, and penalties—would be a very desirable tax. The rabble-rousers were wrong. By the 1890s, the income tax began to look good to most Americans—especially if you could impose it on the rich.

Socialism was also born during this period, and the idea of truly limited government and personal self-reliance began to be replaced with a philosophy of big government, which, of course, required big taxes. Capitalism had produced great inequities and social injustices. Reformers began to see the income tax as the whip to tame the old capitalist monster. Edward Bellamy had written a popular novel, *Looking Backward* (1888), that envisioned

Uncle Sam, with his foot in a mantrap, is shown in Harper's Weekly, 1878, *facing the question, "Will he dare do it?" Will Congress adopt an income tax shown as a chain of bondage around the hardworking citizen and a handout of free whiskey to the shiftless idler? Today, the handout might be food stamps.*

a utopian socialist state. There were "Bellamy Clubs" throughout the nation to discuss and implement his utopian dreams. The income tax and estate tax would be a two-edged sword, by taking wealth from the rich and providing government with the revenue for a socialist state. America did not need the Vanderbilts, the Rockefellers, or J. P. Morgans.

In short, Americans were seduced by the philosophy of socialism, and the liberals still are. Their political agenda is a copy of the agenda of the Socialist Party of America of many years ago. But not all have been seduced, at least not by the end of the twentieth century. A socialist state looks more like George Orwell's *1984* than Bellamy's *Looking Backward*. Big Brother has replaced the nice guys Bellamy had in mind. Radical socialism gave the world communism, and an infinitely wiser world has seen the fruits of that enforced system and wants no part of it. Lately, libertarians and conservatives are drawing us back to the founders' philosophy, to a government with a duty to protect the individual, his property, and his liberty. Not only is this the reason for government, but the limitation of government.

We have learned that Thomas Paine was right when he warned that it is a great mistake to look upon government as some "wonderful mysterious thing." When people believe that illusion, excessive taxes are obtained, just as he predicted. Add to that wisdom his observation that there are two classes of citizens: those who pay taxes and those who live on other people's taxes. When taxes are excessive, you disunite these two classes and set the stage for a revolution in government—for a government less expensive and more productive.

The appeal of socialist philosophy was so overpowering to our fathers at the turn of this century that they abandoned the ideas of the founders, followed the forbidden paths they warned about, and have shackled us at the end of this century with money that is almost worthless compared to the money they inherited—to taxes that are unbelievably oppressive—and to an overblown government that is out of control. We can easily see ourselves heading down a road followed by many great empires of the past that taxed and spent themselves to death. The challenge of our age is not the threat of a foreign invader, but our own tax self-destructiveness. Can we extricate ourselves?

14

"Do Not Dig a Hole for Somebody Else, Lest you Fall in it Yourself"

With the coming of the income tax in America as a permanent, peacetime revenue device, we demonstrated the truth behind a famous Russian proverb used as this chapter's title.

The income tax laws in the nineteenth century applied to everyone. During the Civil War years and in Napoleonic times, the income tax was essentially uniform, with the same or similar rates for all citizens. Then, with the advent of Marxism, high progressive tax rates for the rich were proposed, as a device to destroy capitalism. Finally, in 1894, Congress passed our first peacetime income tax. It was progressive not in its 2 percent rate, but in the fact that it exempted 98 percent of the population, and was simply class legislation against the rich. The idea of taxing only the rich and letting everyone else ride freely on the government was good politics in a democracy, because the vote of the top 2 percent was insignificant. President Clinton used this approach when campaigning for the presidency. He would pay for all his new spending by taxing the top 2 percent, exactly as was the game plan for the income tax of one hundred years ago.

The idea of taxing only the rich and letting everyone else off the

Do not dig a hole for somebody else,
lest you fall in it yourself.

tax hook is a modern political ploy with roots in the past. In America, as with the Russian proverb, a tax that began for the rich ended up putting the income tax on everyone—the middle class ended up in the ditch they had dug for the rich. The monster turned on its creators.

In the congressional debates over taxes during the Civil War, a congressman related this story:

> The tax was very much like a boil that a man had on his nose. He complained very much about it being there, and his friend asked, "Where else would you want to have it?" He thought for a while and then answered, "Well, I believe I would rather have it on some other man's back."

That humorous story is very profound, for it is a good summary of what tax history has been about—for the past five thousand years of recorded history. It vividly demonstrates what the framers tried to avoid by making taxes "uniform" throughout the nation, or, as they said during the debates, "common to all." Not a bad idea; too bad it has not survived to our times.

The Supreme Court quickly got involved in the 1894 income tax law. The case was the most celebrated one of the period. The reports on the hearings and rehearings would almost fill a volume. In the end, the majority of the justices found the tax unconstitutional. It was, in part, a direct tax and therefore had to be apportioned among the states by population. The Court was divided on the question of uniformity, although Justice Stephen Field wrote a concurring opinion declaring that the tax lacked uniformity in exempting 98 percent of the population: "Under wise and constitutional legislation, every citizen should contribute his proportion, however small the sum, to the support of government, and it is no kindness to urge any of our citizens to escape this obligation."

There was a dissenting opinion by Justice John Harlan, who has given us the famous phrase, "The Constitution is color-blind," as the lone dissent in the segregation case of that era. Harlan believed the income tax law before the Court was not a form of direct taxation, hence it need not be apportioned. But he was sensitive to the "uniform" requirement of the Constitution, and said that exemptions were most liable to objection, and the government could not use taxation as a means of legislative plunder. Tax exemptions were "dangerous," he said. Today, of course, that's only history.

Some of the lawyers' arguments were amazingly prophetic, although not intended to be. For example, one lawyer argued that if the rate was 2 percent today, it might conceivably be 20 percent tomorrow, i.e., plunder. No one even suggested it might be over 90 percent tomorrow—that would have been laughed out of court as absurdity. But tax laws that are productive of revenue have a tendency to become absurd, as we have witnessed with our income and estate tax laws. Another lawyer made an even more profound and prophetic observation:

> the fundamental principle at stake was whether or not the United States would be a land of equality in taxation, for once it is decided that the many can tax the few, it will be impossible to take a backward step.

This of course was Madison's problem as we noted in chapter 7. The 1894 income tax case called *Pollock* v. *Farmer Loan and Trust*

Co. has misled taxpayers into believing that Congress was bound to enact "wise and constitutional tax legislation," a phrase from Justice Field's opinion. But, as the years passed, and with the Sixteenth Amendment, which authorized income taxes without any apportionment, it became increasingly clear that the Court wanted no more challenges to tax laws, and that Congress could tax at its pleasure. As the nineteenth century came to a close, the Court began abandoning its role as guardian of the Constitution so far as federal tax laws were concerned. As tax laws became increasingly abusive and even discriminatory, lacking even a semblance of uniformity, the Court washed its hands of them.

At the time the income tax debate was raging, the idea of progressive tax rates came before the High Court. In 1899, the Court approved progressive tax rates with this absurd comment:

> The grave consequences which it is asserted must arise in the future if the right to levy a progressive tax be recognized involves in its ultimate aspect the mere assertion that free and representative government is a failure, and that the grossest abuses of power are foreshadowed.

The Court's reasoning proved to be ridiculous within eight years of the first progressive income tax in 1913. By 1921, the top rate had escalated from 7 percent to 77 percent, eventually rising in peacetime to over 90 percent. Moreover, progressive death taxes increased to 70 percent. Madison warned, in *The Federalists* (1788), about the "temptation" in taxmaking for the majority to "trample on the rules of justice," by overtaxing a minority without political clout. His prediction came to pass dramatically when the Supreme Court tossed the uniformity command out the window.

The founders believed strongly in the principle of apportionment; that is, taxes had to be apportioned among the people by some definite, nonarbitrary standard. But progressive rates, at the whim of the Congress, involve no principle whatsoever. At work is the Marxian concept of "ability to pay," based on arbitrary powers to discriminate against the rich. In essence, the "ability to pay"

This French engraving on the eve of the French Revolution portrays the injustices of tax exemptions within the French social order. The uniformity command in the Constitution was designed at that time to prevent this from happening in American society, where taxes were to be "common to all."

became the government's word for stealing. The legendary thief Robin Hood justified his thievery on the same premise. Worse still, the battle cry of the American Revolution of taxation by consent became a fraud. Even the village idiot knows no one consents to a discriminatory tax, not fairly apportioned among the people. The working principle of a truly democratic society is that a law, to be just, must give equal treatment to all. In the final analysis, the "ability to pay," backed by police power, is just rank extortion.

"Extortion" is not a nice word. It does have, however, a long and interesting history with regard to taxation. The British government in the seventeenth century recorded a substantial amount of revenue from "Extortions." It meant taxpayers who paid a tax to which they did not consent, and who were discriminated against. These Treasury records are referring to the tax known as "decima-

Supreme Court Justice Stephen Field, who wrote in his concurring opinion in the 1895 income tax case that the "sure decadence of our government will commence" if the Court ever sanctions tax discrimination "and nullifies the uniformity command of the Constitution." Was he right?

tions," which was a 10 percent tax on all those loyal to King Charles I. It was a tax on the "Loyalist," which was not levied against Cromwell's followers, since after beheading the king and setting up their "Commonwealth," they were running the government and the tax bureau.

Extortion is a sister word to "exaction," from the Latin *exactio*, meaning "to tax." While exaction means "to force out," extortion, literally, means "to twist out." When the British first adopted progressive tax rates in 1894, Congress also adopted a peacetime income tax. *The Times* in London attacked the idea of progressive tax rates, citing Adam Smith. It wrote: "When the rule of arithmetical proportion is broken, the door is open to extortion." William Blackstone, in his great *Commentaries* (1:136), calls exactions (taxes) without real and genuine consent "extortions." There seems little doubt that our progressive tax rates, if levied without real and genuine consent on those who bear the increased rate, are extortions, whether we like the term or not.

15

"A Perfect System of Espionage"

Proponents of income tax in America were able to offer seventy years of British experience as strong proof that the tax would not destroy liberty and bring tyranny. Fears of an overbearing bureaucracy fueled American opposition to income tax. Britain's relative success with it showed that the tax, if properly administered, would not endanger American liberty.

Opponents of income tax had argued that such a tax was "defensible [only] on the same ground the highwayman defends his acts, socialists with their schemes, and anarchists with their bombs." But as the debate continued, the tide began to turn. One professor, Edwin Seligman, in 1911 wrote a scholarly treatise, *The Income Tax,* which greatly helped the cause of the Sixteenth Amendment. In dealing with the fears of tyranny, he wrote, "Early complaints against the inquisitorial character of the tax have long since well-nigh completely disappeared." In 1911, that was a very reasonable position. Like the excise, the income tax could be good or bad, depending on its acceptance by the people and its administration in a free society. History had proven that the rabble-rousers were wrong, dead wrong, so it seemed.

There was, however, at that time a current income tax in Germany, and it was tyrannical. How could Americans be sure their income tax would mimic Britain's and not Germany's? The German system was called tyrannical because of its administrative procedures: the auditing methods of German tax authorities—and the obligation of all taxpayers to declare and pay their tax, rather than having it withheld at the source. German tax surveillance was so extensive that one German legislator declared "The country is covered with a perfect system of espionage."

But the German income tax system did not bother Professor Seligman. It was an aberration that could not happen here. Said the learned professor:

> Such an inquisitorial system would be impracticable almost anywhere else . . . nowhere else are the people so meek in the face of officialdom. In no other country in the world would it be possible to enforce so inquisitional a procedure as we have learned to be customary in Prussia.

If the German income tax a hundred years ago was a perfect system of espionage, then today, with all our high-tech intrusions into everything imaginable, ours is a superperfect system. But the history of how America went from an honor system to a spy system is recent. It took place only over the past few decades. Here is the scenario:

Thirty-five years ago I was a freshman attorney on my first audit. An IRS agent of some years looked across the desk where I was sitting and said, "You know, our tax system is an honor system, which is the only way it will work in a free society." I don't know if that was his personal sales pitch, or if that was the training the IRS gave to all agents. But in my case it made good sense, and I am sure he was very successful in putting our tax system upon an "honor system." Some of the top brass at the IRS also spoke in a similar vein. At this same time, IRS Commissioner Mortimer

Caplin wrote that "No other nation in the world has ever equaled this record [of voluntary compliance]. It is a tribute to our people, their tradition of honesty, and their high sense of responsibility in supporting our government." (1962)

A few years before that, Robert Jackson, the chief counsel for the IRS, who later became a Supreme Court justice, said:

> The United States has a system of taxation by confession. That a people so numerous, scattered and individualistic annually assesses itself with a tax liability often in highly burdensome amounts, is a reassuring sign of stability and vitality of our system of government.

More recently, the tune changed dramatically. In 1982, Justice Richard Neely wrote in *Atlantic* magazine that "Cheating on federal and state income tax is all pervasive in all classes of society; except among the compulsively honest, cheating usually occurs in direct proportion to opportunity."

Even more recently (1996) one of America's most respected journalists, David Brinkley, said almost the same thing as Justice Neely:

> The American people as taxpayers have begun in wholesale numbers to cheat, out of resentment of a tax system they think is unfair, too complicated and wasteful of their money. The so-called underground economy is growing rapidly—people working for cash only, reporting nothing, paying nothing.

Both Brinkley and Justice Neely are bringing to light and into focus our latest tax rebellion. What neither suspects, is that this is a revival of a long dormant spirit of tax defiance that was once a part of the American character, and it is doubtful that for the government—no matter how draconian and totalitarian its response—the revolt will not go away until the tax law is changed.

WHAT HAS HAPPENED in the twenty years between Commissioner Caplin's and Justice Neely's views? We have moved with each Congress and each new piece of tax legislation away from an honor system into a spy system. It may have been fully justified if Justice Neely is correct. It shows a broad tax revolt against the income tax system. We have witnessed the emigration of the rich, and that is apparent by recent tax legislation trying to punish anyone who gives up his or her citizenship to avoid tax. There have to be tens of thousands of wealthy Americans who have left the United States to avoid tax. Historically, flight to avoid tax has been the best and safest way to rebel, and it still is. Where do they go? Recently, the General Accounting Office (GAO) said that over a million American citizens living in Europe had filed no tax returns. New regulations have come forth to try to bring these tax evaders back into the fold when they want to get their passports renewed. (Part of the passport procedure requires a nonresident American to notify the IRS of his or her whereabouts.)

The underground economy offers some relief for a few, but not too many people can remove themselves from the all-seeing eye of the taxman. Just about everything you do of a fiscal nature is reported on some ubiquitous "information" return. President Clinton found it almost impossible to appoint a woman as U.S. Attorney General if she had children. Payments to baby-sitters require reporting to the taxman, and in the course of the life of almost any mother, she will have hired a baby-sitter whose small fees slipped by Big Brother.

What is the meaning behind the almost universal inclination to evade our income tax? The meaning is simple: it is a clear sign of a tax revolt—a nonviolent tax revolt, but a revolt nevertheless. Four hundred years ago, when Imperial Spain was confronted with massive tax evasion throughout the empire, the government did exactly what our government has done, as described by a modern Spanish historian:

Spanish industry was strangled by the most burdensome and complicated system of taxation that human folly can devise. The taxpayer,

overburdened with imposts, was entangled with a network of regulations to prevent evasion. . . . He was thus crippled at every step by the
deadly influence of the anomalous and incongruous accumulation of
exactions.

It is amazing how well this description of Spanish tax policy
against evading Spaniards fits our current tax policy against American inclination to evade. Are we not "entangled with a network of
regulations to prevent evasion," from "the anomalous and incongruous accumulation of exactions"? Spain's network of "regulations to
prevent evasion" was enforced with death penalties, which failed to
stop the evasions. Many other tax bureaus in the past have also used
the death penalty and, in addition, instruments of torture, both with
the same unsatisfactory results—the evasion continued, nevertheless.

Today, we manufacture synthetic felonies to terrorize taxpayers—tax crimes which are vague and fuzzy and easily applicable to
any erring taxpayer. What is happening here, as in the past, is that
you cannot legislate against human nature, and when taxpayers believe they are being unjustly treated, they will rebel in one form or
another: violence or emigration or evasion, whatever is available at
the time. Montesquieu warned that when taxes are excessive, governments will have to resort to "extraordinary means of oppression." We can see that prediction today, in the United States more
than in any other nation.

To check the defiant American taxpayer, we have moved from
an honor system to a spy system in the last twenty-five years,
backed up with draconian punishments.

If you doubt our punishments are savage, you should consider
a thirty-year prison term given to a woman, Trula Walker, by a
Kansas City federal judge, Dean Whipple. There are other examples, such as an Oregon high school coach who got twenty-five
years, with no reduction. Leona Helmsley cheated on less than 1
percent of her taxes, yet at seventy-one years, with no criminal
record, she got four years in prison. These psychopathic punish-

ments are Montesquieu's "extraordinary means of oppression." In *The Wealth of Nations,* Adam Smith actually excused tax evasions, and so did both Blackstone and Montesquieu. Said Smith: "Where there is at least a general suspicion of much unnecessary expense, and great misapplication of the public revenue, the laws which guard it are little respected." Smith said the tax evader is "in every respect, an excellent citizen, had not the laws of his country made a crime which nature never meant to be so." William Blackstone in his *Commentaries* said that making tax evasion a felony "destroys all proportion of punishment, and puts murders upon equal footing with such as are really guilty of no natural, but merely a positive offense."

When the United States was struggling to adopt an income tax, so were the French. They, too, took notice of the Prussian system as an aberration, but just like Professor Seligman, they thought it could not happen in France. The French minister of finance, upon submitting an income tax law to the National Assembly, said not to worry, as the French government would not grant to the French tax bureau the "exorbitant powers" enjoyed by the Prussian tax ministry.

Of course, the "inquisitional procedure," or the "exorbitant powers" in operation in Prussia, or the "perfect system of espionage," is what both France and the United States have in force today, with the United States topping all tax bureaus for Prussian-type tax operations. And we wonder why people don't trust their politicians, especially their taxmakers. Once the taxman is allowed to put his foot in your door, history will show that you can expect it to be followed by a bulldozer.

When the British government in 1894 introduced progressive tax rates for death duties, the chancellor of the exchequer made it clear there was nothing to worry about with regard to income taxes, as no progressive rates would be allowed for income taxes; otherwise, the evils would be intolerable. He explained to the House of Commons:

There is no inquisitional prying into the ways and means of each individual. You do not demand the sight of his cash book or his pass book but the tax is deducted in the majority of cases from the income before it reaches him . . . measures of penal discovery and irritating inquisition which requires the determination of every man's income from all sources would render the collection of the Income Tax so odious as to imperil its existence and in all probability make it impossible to maintain the tax.

But the opposition wasn't deceived. As one MP replied to the chancellor:

But where are you going to find a standard of what is right to take? . . . I think the standard will vary from Parliament to Parliament and from majority to majority; and the principle of taxation will depend on the wave of public opinion, and not on equality of taxation which has been insisted upon in our finances. . . . I am anxious that this graduation should not become a kind of *scaffolding for plunder* . . . there is the possibility of inflicting injustice after injustice because you will have no standard to guide you and no landmarks to place along this road of taxation.

Fifteen years later, in 1909, a new British leadership was arguing for progressive income taxes, a "supertax," as it was called. The prime minister, Lloyd George, argued to the Commons that the proposed progressive rates were "quite gentle," and were perfectly fair, just an extra 2½ percent on top of a flat 5 percent. No big deal. But the German system was still a worry to many a Briton and Frenchman. The prime minister said not to worry, "In Germany the whole of the income is submitted, there is a system of investigation which probably we would not stand in this country; it is a very severe one. We do not propose anything of that kind here."

Once the floodgates were open to progressive rates, the rates soon accelerated to almost complete confiscation, and they did apply to the "whole of income." The "quite gentle" tax rates became brutally severe, and the German system became the order of the day in Britain, France, and the United States. In short, the benign British income tax of the nineteenth century became a monster.

16

"The Detestable Race of Informers"

The Roman emperor Constantine made a decree in A.D. 313 condemning the "race of informers" in Roman legal proceedings:

> The greatest scourge of mankind, the detestable race of tax informers, must be stopped. We must stifle it in its first efforts and tear out the pernicious tongue of envy. Let not the judges receive . . . information of the informer; let them be given up to punishment as soon as any of them appear.

In ancient Rome, the use of informers got out of hand, and their testimony became false and unreliable, so much so that the government had to reverse itself and root out the "detestable race of informers," which suggests a substantial economic class of citizens who supported themselves by informing on others and collecting the rewards. The decree of Constantine is the first evidence we have of an exclusionary rule of evidence, which we use today for the purpose of deterring illegal searches. In Rome, it was to deter informers, and the false testimony they were likely to produce.

Informers are not used in the modern world except in the United States. Like the informers in the ancient world, U.S. informers receive a percentage of the tax recovered. It is ironic that the United States pursues a policy of promoting informers, when the American Revolution was sparked by a similar practice instituted by British revenue authorities in the 1760s and 1770s.

We first discover informers in the Old Testament, when the Jews were under Egyptian tribute. In the Book of Ecclesiastes, Judea is described as a land of tax informers. The spies of the pharaoh were everywhere, we are told, so that "a bird of the air shall carry the voice" of any Jew who cursed the king. It was the king's tax burdens that the Jews were cursing.

In Rome's better days, we learn of an unusual type of informer against Roman taxmen, so that if a taxman collected more than was due, the informer received part of the penalty assessed for the excessive collection. These were unusual times, for civil and criminal fines were assessed against taxmen who collected more than the law required. Could you imagine, today, civil fines against federal tax agents who collected or attempted to collect more than the tax law permitted? Yet that was the practice during Rome's better days. Is there not a lesson here for us?

Payment for informing on your fellow taxpayer is part of the Internal Revenue Code, and there are special training sessions to show agents how to enlist people to inform on their friends, neighbors, employers—even family members. It is all reminiscent of the Soviet Union, where children were taught by parents that "the walls have ears." A statue was even built in one Soviet city honoring a child who informed on his parents. Hopefully, the IRS won't go that far. The fact that this whole IRS operation of informers is sub rosa to a large extent indicates some sense of bureaucratic guilt for this evil practice. The fact that no other nation promotes tax informers suggests that the practice is hardly compatible with the temper of a free people. Collecting revenue is important, but is it so important as to promote a "detestable race of informers"?

The most insidious informers today are not people, but paper—the ubiquitous "information" return, which all citizens are required to file on fiscal activities of others to let the government know just about everything about you that might possibly involve taxes. The worst victims are the banks, and huge penalties have been levied against some of our biggest banks for not informing on customers that use cash or engage in many kinds of transactions the taxman wants to know about. Again, like the paid informers, the United States is the only country in the world that engages in such compulsory "informing" on just about everything imaginable. Even the barest of banking privacy has no place in America. Your banking records are not just an open book, they are a family photo album as well.

When it comes to spying and snooping into the financial affairs of citizens, America is the world's leader, if that is anything to brag about. Consider the Bank Secrecy Act, which is a misnomer, it is really a Bank *No* Secrecy Act. Everything going through your bank account is photographed and held for Big Brother to see. The Supreme Court upheld this practice because it might be "useful" for tax enforcement. In what will undoubtedly be seen as one of the great dissenting opinions, ranking with those of Brandeis and Holmes, Justice William O. Douglas replied to Justice Rehnquist's "useful" logic:

> It would be highly useful to governmental espionage to have like reports from all our bookstores, all our hardware and retail stores, all our drugstores. These records too might be "useful" in criminal investigations. . . . A mandatory recording of all telephone conversations would be better than the recording of checks under the Bank Secrecy Act, if Big Brother is to have his way.

This case, which is called the *California Bankers' Association* case (1974), had to deal with these words from a case in 1885, *Boyd* v.

United States, which struck down a tax law that required taxpayers to bring in their records for examination:

> And any compulsory discovery by extorting the party's oath, or compelling the production of his private books and papers, to convict him of a crime, or to forfeit his property, is contrary to the principles of a free government. It is abhorrent to the instincts of an Englishman; it is abhorrent to the instincts of an American. It may suit the purposes of despotic power; but it cannot abide the pure atmosphere of political liberty and personal freedom.

Louis Brandeis is on every list of great Supreme Court justices. Most of his brilliant dissents became law. In one of his most famous dissents, he referred to the *Boyd* case as a ruling that "will be remembered as long as civil liberties live in the United States." The *Boyd* case has been cited more than three thousand times in the past hundred years, but not for protecting our civil liberties. It took the first woman on the Supreme Court to acknowledge that the Court had "sounded the death knell for *Boyd.*" In doing so, so often, was not the Court also sounding the death knell for a large bundle of our civil liberties?

The Court has become basically anti-*Boyd,* with Chief Justice Rehnquist the leader of the gravediggers. On June 20, 1986, the *New York Times* prophetically observed that with his appointment as Chief Justice: "We could have a different country, one in which our freedoms are less secure, official power less restrained." Polite words to describe judicial tolerance for fascism.

Banking privacy is a fundamental liberty throughout most of the free world. It is not just a Swiss practice. It is rooted in the ancient principle that a man's castle is beyond the surveillance of the king. And what was in the castle that the owner wanted kept from the king's snooping? It was his treasury, not his chickens and goats. Once the king knew about the castle treasury, he was apt to find a way to plunder it.

In Switzerland, banking privacy is not absolute, as a number of

American crooks have discovered. But most important, privacy is not for foreigners or Americans, but it exists for the Swiss people. They don't want their government snooping into their bank accounts without real cause. No fishing expeditions. As one Swiss apologist explains:

> Banking secrecy is a major component of the wall of discretion that must protect the individual with his privacy if liberty is to be defended with success against the dominance of the state. This, and no less, is what is at stake. The frightening thing is that it should be necessary to state it.

Though Switzerland has an almost foolproof system of banking privacy for everything except common crimes, it also can boast of substantial compliance with its income tax laws. And among European nations, Switzerland is not gentle with its tax sinners, although it has nothing like the savage punishments meted out to Americans for their tax sins.

Even the executive branch of the Swiss government recognizes that its banking privacy is the will and wishes of the Swiss people, not the government itself. I have always felt that if the American people, or any people for that matter, were given a vote on whether or not to have privacy for their banking and finances from a snooping Big Brother tax bureaucracy, the vote would almost be unanimous. Here is what the top leadership in the Swiss government, Roger Bouvin, of the Swiss Federal Council, like our president and cabinet, had to say in 1967: "In the view of the Swiss people, the freedom of the individual takes precedence over the fiscal interests [of the state], even on the risk that this freedom is sometimes misused."

Note it's the "Swiss people" who are responsible for banking privacy. One wonders what the American people would want, if they had their say? All the countries of Western civilization, the so-called free countries, have banking privacy laws. Only in America, and in various police states, can the government snoop at will. Does that tell us something?

On the lighter side, it is amazing how thieves and robbers have misunderstood banking secrecy. A number of very well-planned robberies, in the millions, have put the robbers in prison when they whisked off their loot to a bank secrecy country, only to find themselves on a flight back to the USA, in handcuffs, attached to an FBI agent.

This misunderstanding comes from Hollywood movies. Film writers like to show Swiss and Cayman Islands bankers as eager participants in accepting stolen money. This was dramatized in the movie *The Thomas Crown Affair*. Steve McQueen plays the part of Thomas Crown, a super-successful tycoon who has become bored with life. To add excitement to his boredom, he plans and pulls off a series of brilliant bank heists, and deposits his loot in a Swiss bank.

In the final scene, he is on a Swissair flight to Geneva. Below is Faye Dunaway, playing the tenacious insurance investigator, whose quarry has just slipped from her grasp on the airliner headed for Switzerland. Steve McQueen had masterminded another heist. He looks out at the skyline of Boston with a sly smile on his face, for he knows what Faye Dunaway must be thinking as he eludes her trap. In Geneva he will retrieve his stolen cash, which he had deposited in a Swiss bank under a numbered account with a false name, and live happily ever after on his hot loot. Actually, in the real world he would have been arrested by the Swiss police at the airport, and in short order would be on a return flight to the United States, in handcuffs, for prosecution.

In the Cayman Islands, shortly after this movie, a group of bank robbers almost duplicated the Thomas Crown game plan. But they *did* find themselves on a chartered airplane handcuffed to FBI agents. The error the movie made was to depict banking privacy countries as havens for thieves. They are not. There is no such thing as an "assumed name bank account" or an anonymous numbered account. It makes great fiction for a movie, but it is not reality.

The numbered account was developed to foil attempts by Nazi fiscal investigators trying to locate Jewish accounts in Switzerland. Hitler had instituted special taxes against the Jews to destroy Jewish wealth and power in Germany. To evade these taxes, Jewish money was smuggled across the border and deposited in banks, most often in Zurich or Basel. Swiss bank clerks had been known to take bribes. Another device to breach the banking secrecy was for the Nazi investigator to try to make a deposit in the name of the suspected Jewish account. If the deposit was accepted, that proved the existence of the account. By introducing the numbered account, the tellers did not know the name of the depositor, but the name was known by the managerial staff. This is all there is to the so-called numbered account. To add further protection, the Swiss made it a felony to attempt to breach their secrecy. Even today, foreign agents are sometimes caught trying to penetrate the Swiss banking system.

Americans, like others, benefit from Swiss banking practices. A new Big Brother has replaced the Nazis. He, too, is watching.

17

Fiscal Whiz-kids or Nitwits?
Or, You Can Never Accuse the
Government of Being Smart

Wise men will not always be at the helm.

—James Madison, *The Federalist No. 10*

Madison warned that with respect to taxmaking, wise men would not always be at the helm; our experience has been worse than he predicted. Nitwits and fools seem to have been our misfortune. Stupidity may be an even better description, as our taxmen show complete obliviousness to the past and the calamities excessive taxing and spending have brought other nations. The government's greed has put tax collection above all else, without considering the ethical consequences. When citizens rebel by evading or emigrating, Congress responds by passing more ugly laws. Maybe they should consider what Diocletian did to prevent Romans from packing their bags and leaving town. He ordered everyone to stay where they were and chained them to their jobs or farms. It was very effective—a mild form of slavery for the once free Romans—but justified to ensure the collection of taxes. Of course, we don't have to do that. With tax-identifying numbers and a myriad of information returns, we know where everyone is and what they are doing, taxwise. If Diocletian were around, he'd probably ask himself, why didn't I think of that?

It was once firmly believed that shirking your duty to pay taxes was the sign of a poor citizen. Today, not engaging in all the legal tax gamesmanship possible is the sign of a damn fool. The tax law doesn't even try to allocate the cost of government among the wealth and income of the nation by some fair standard. Multimillionaires like Howard Hughes didn't pay any income taxes because of tax exemptions, but why riddle the tax code with exemptions? We don't exempt people from the criminal law; why exempt people from the tax law? Of course, in the end Hughes lost. The death tax took most of his wealth.

Every tax exemption or even tax inequality has a powerful group of followers with political clout. But the biggest problem, as old as civilization, is that when governments spend too much, they will resort to anything that fills their spending pot, even stealing or plundering. Perhaps the greatest of the tax thieves was old "Bluff King Hal," also known as King Henry VIII. When he ran short of cash, and Parliament refused to grant him new revenues and rebuked him for instituting taxes without parliamentary consent, he looked around England for some wealth to steal, and noticed the great estates owned by the monasteries and the churches. As the newly declared head of the Church of England, he proceeded to confiscate all Church lands and buildings in England, unquestionably one of the greatest heists of all time. A number of problems developed, however. One was the matter of charity for the poor, the sick, the orphans, and the homeless. The monasteries took care of them, and with their land confiscated, what was to become of these unfortunates? No problem, said Hal, just order the local parishes and villages to provide shelter and care for them. Henry obviously wanted his newly stolen property free from all encumbrances.

The "bluff" part of his nickname came from his newly minted

coinage. It soon became about 60 percent base metal, whether gold or silver. In other words, he did what Jimmy Carter and his whiz-kids did to America some twenty years ago. Henry's heist also has a counterpart—fleece a wealthy class without any political clout. Other kings in Europe had routinely fleeced their Jewish subjects with extortionate taxation, so Hal was now fleecing the Catholic Church. Today, we have tried to do the same thing to our wealthy classes with 90-plus percent tax rates on income and 70 percent rates at death (today a mere 55 percent). Like the Jews in the Middle Ages or the Catholic Church in England, the dead have little political clout.

An important historical counterpart of our taxes can be found in the *alcabala,* the 10 percent excise tax in Imperial Spain. No matter how bad, how destructive it was, it was never in danger of being repealed, because it was such a moneymaker. A modern Spanish historian made this observation: "The alcabala became the most lucrative of all taxes . . . hence the tenacity with which many generations of Castilian kings clung to this disastrous impost." With the change of only a couple of words, this condemnation of the *alcabala* would easily apply to our clinging to our disastrous impost, the income tax.

Consider William Gladstone, who was prime minister of Great Britain, off and on, for fifty years during the latter half of the nineteenth century. He professed strong contempt for the income tax, yet could not get rid of it. Here are his words in 1853 in the debates in the Commons over a three-year extension of the income tax:

> The public feeling of its inequality is a fact most important in itself. The inquisition it entails is a most serious disadvantage, and the frauds to which it leads are an evil such as it is not possible to characterize in terms too strong.

Remember, Gladstone was writing when the income tax was a flat 3 percent; and as the rates have escalated in our century, the evils have magnified even more so. Gladstone's inability to abolish income taxation as British prime minister should help us to understand why we can't, either. The culprit, explained Gladstone, was the "public expenditure," and the abandonment of the "spirit of thrift in government." As long as we have an overblown and overspending government, an income tax is probably inevitable, as it is a great engine for producing revenue.

Liberty suffered, said Gladstone, because the collection of great revenues requires an army of tax officials with great powers. In such a situation, the delights of spending money—taxpayers' money—cause politicians to lean toward the tax official who butters their bread rather than toward the taxpayer who produces the butter.

Today, politicians are much worse than in Gladstone's time, because what they can't get by taxes, they can get by borrowing. This puts the tax bill off on our great-grandchildren, plus a few more generations to come.

Recently, we have awakened with a shock to our public debt and continuing deficits. We have yet to realize just how deep that debt is, and how bad our politicians have been in managing government finances. It is not unlikely that our children in the next two centuries will look back upon us with great contempt—first, for the destruction of the environment in so many ways, especially with radiation poisoning that will take thousands of years to dissipate; and second, for the astronomical debt we pass on to them. They will have every right to hate us; especially when so many other prosperous nations, notably in Asia, will be leaving their children a full treasury, free from debt.

Our descendants will inherit a debt almost beyond human capacity to conceive. So large (about $4 trillion) that if we paid it off at the rate of the daily costs of the O. J. Simpson trial (estimated at $55,000 a day), it would take over 250,000 years to discharge that debt; 100,000 years just to pay the current (1995) budget. That would take us through three or four ice ages. At the rate we are going, our descendants may end up with a national debt that, at the rate of $55,000 a day, would take them back in time to the age of the dinosaurs! Steve Moore of the Cato Institute in Washington, D.C., gives this example in the *Wall Street Journal:*

> Try this one on for size. Imagine a train of 50 foot boxcars with $1 bills. How long would the train have to be to carry the 1.6 Trillion Congress spends each year? About $65 million can be stuffed in one boxcar. The train would have to be 240 miles long to carry enough dollar bills to balance the federal budget. In other words, the train would stretch from Washington, through Baltimore, Delaware, Philadelphia, New Jersey, and into New York City.

How do we extricate ourselves from this fiscal mess? From a tax system that has gone bad and a debt obligation that is out of this world? Does history provide any clues?

After the War of Independence, the Americans found that taxation with representation was much worse than taxation without representation—mainly because they had incurred an enormous war debt. Rather than repudiate the war debt or try to pay it off with cheap money, Alexander Hamilton insisted the federal government take over the war debts of the states and that they be paid with sound money. From that day on, over two hundred years ago, the credit of the United States has been sound and recognized as safe. Only recently have we decided to repay our national debts with cheap money.

The founders had an enormous war debt, and considering their limited resources, it may provide a lesson for us, as all fiscal matters are relevant. It took the United States over fifty years to repay the national debt and get the government out of the red. In 1834, the national debt was finally paid, from obligations initially incurred at the founding, when the Revolutionary War ended.

So maybe it will take us fifty years to repay our debts, but that would not appear necessary. Canada, for example, had a huge war debt after World War II, yet repaid the debt after less than ten years. Canada's debt today, which on an adjusted basis is actually less than the war debt, will not be so easy to repay any more than the United States' debt. The reason?

War debts diminish when wars end. Our military costs have been kept unusually high because of the cold war, plus a couple of hot wars along the way (Korea and Vietnam). But now that the cold war is over, and military expenditures are down, our huge deficit spending continues. To duplicate the road to solvency after World War II, as in Canada, we would have to get out from under two heavy burdens: First, from the welfare state, the Santa Claus state, or better still, the sucker state. Those eating from the public trough will have to find another means of support—like self-reliance, an old national virtue. The tax system is only half the problem. Is not Gladstone right in pointing out the problem of abandoning the spirit of thrift in government? For the second problem is what we can call the "fat paycheck" problem. Those working for the federal government, including contractors, who require a fat paycheck. Whatever became of unselfish service for one's country?

In early Rome, government service, from the highest magistrates to the soldiers in the legions, was performed without any pay. This practice catapulted Rome into leadership over the entire ancient world. So much so, that historians at that time considered the spirit of unselfish service to be the *sine qua non* of Rome's rise to power—something that was totally lacking from the Greeks, as Greece declined and Rome took over. The Greek historian Polybius gives us this insight into Roman public servants as compared to Greek public servants:

> Among the Greeks, apart from anything else, men who hold public office cannot be trusted . . . even if they have ten accountants . . . whereas among the Romans their magistrates handle large sums of money and scrupulously perform their duty. . . . Among other nations

INFLATION BY THE BUSHEL, ROMAN STYLE

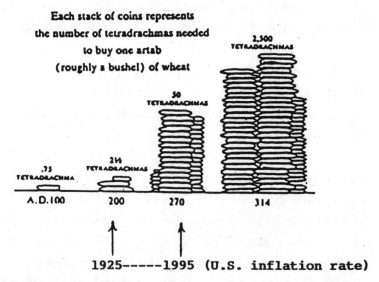

Each stack of coins represents
the number of tetradrachmas needed
to buy one artab
(roughly a bushel) of wheat

2,500 TETRADRACHMAS

50 TETRADRACHMAS

.75 TETRADRACHMA

2¼ TETRADRACHMAS

A.D. 100   200   270   314

1925-----1995 (U.S. inflation rate)

The U.S. inflation rate from 1925 to 1995 (seventy years) was identical to the Roman in-flation rate from A.D. 200 to 270. Shouldn't that tell us something? Ring some bells? For the people it does, but not for the whiz-kids at the Treasury. They don't want to talk about it.

it is a rare phenomenon to find a man who keeps his hands off public funds . . . while among the Romans it is quite the exception to find a man who has been detected in such conduct. (ca. 125 B.C.)

So, not only did the Romans work for nothing in state service, they also were men of great honor and integrity. Can we find such men and women for our public service?

The final nail in our coffin will probably be our increasingly worthless money. We are right on course with what the later Romans did in exactly the same time frame, no less. The above illustration, "Inflation by the bushel," could be our Roman tragedy.

The Roman fiscal whiz-kids added base metals to the once pure drachma. This was easier than borrowing money or increasing taxes. For example, if the government's spending was 120 percent of tax receipts, then 20 percent of cheap metal would be added to the coinage to bring it up to cover the shortfall in funds. Rather clever, wouldn't you say? In seventy years from A.D. 200 to 270, this produced an inflation of 2,000 percent. It took 50 tetradrachmas to buy a bushel of wheat in 270, while seventy years before, in 200, it took only 2.5 tetradrachmas.

We have done exactly the same thing in the same time frame. In 1925, a nickel (5¢) would buy as much as a dollar (100¢) will buy today, again 2,000 percent inflation. Is our future going to coincide with the rest of the Roman story?

Our inflation really gathered steam when Nixon took us off a modified gold standard. Now, there is no natural restraint against printing more money. We don't add base metals as the Romans did, nor do we let the presses roll as the Germans did, or as the Russians are now doing. We are more clever. Our Federal Reserve creates credits for member banks, in effect creating more money, and thereby increasing the money supply, which increases the cost of goods. We can only hope that the rest of the Roman fiscal calamity is not a course we will follow.

We should learn from the Swiss.

Shortly after Nixon took America off a gold standard, a fiscal expert from the Swiss National Bank commented that the dollar, which was 4:1 for the Swiss franc, would eventually become 1:1. That prediction has almost come to pass today. Why? The Swiss fiscal authorities are limited in the amount of money they can create—limited by the amount of gold on deposit with the National Bank. That prevents the presses from running, or a central bank, like our Fed, from creating great increases in the money supply.

Another protective device of the Swiss is a 35 percent tax on foreigners receiving interest from Swiss government bonds and from deposits in Swiss banks. That way only Swiss citizens can buy these bonds or maintain interest-bearing bank deposits. With such a limited number of borrowers, the Swiss government can't borrow from abroad or from banks at home, thus preventing an overspending or borrowing Swiss government. This is obviously better than the hope for a balanced budget. How, then, you may wonder, do Swiss banks attract so much foreign money—foreign depositors seeking a safe haven? These foreign-owned Swiss bank accounts deposit foreign depositors' money in banks outside Switzerland. Thus, an account in Geneva will deposit its foreign source funds in a bank in the Netherlands, London, the Bahamas, and so on, but not in Switzerland.

Backing currency with gold is considered an outmoded, silly, archaic practice by the whiz-kids in Washington, London, and Toronto. If so, then why have all sound money systems in history had gold or silver behind the currency? And why, when so many financial panics occurred throughout the centuries, was worthless money behind the fiascos, like that of John Law, the fiscal whiz-kid, the man of the hour in early eighteenth-century France? What about his paper money and his Mississippi Bubble? In fact, the history of government finance and fiscal follies, including our own "panics," involves one bubble after another.

On the positive side, take England's rise to superpower status after Henry VIII's fiscal insanity. What happened? His wise and brilliant daughter, Good Queen Bess, called in all her father's debased coinage, and exchanged all the adulterated money for good gold and silver coinage. It took almost all the money she had, plus an enormous loan from the city of Antwerp, which took her a long time to repay. Yet she restored the value of English money, so that the "pound" contained no less than one pound of silver—that's how the pound got its name. England's rulers protected the coinage for three centuries, and British money—the pound sterling—was the most sought after coinage during the era of Britain's greatness. In this century, the British government went back to the "Bluff King Hal" system and debased the coinage after three hundred years. Britain went into a sharp decline. Just a coincidence?

Today, in America, many of our fiscal experts like a weak dollar and amazingly see a strong dollar as a threat to prosperity. If that is so, then shouldn't Switzerland be the poorest country on earth? An economic basket case?

I SHOULD NOT LEAVE the Swiss story without a passing comment on their constitution, which has a tenth amendment provision just like ours. The national government has only those powers expressly given to it. So, when the government wants to do something not set forth expressly in the constitution, they have to go to the voters for an amendment. We, by contrast, go to the Supreme Court, which gives Congress carte blanche. Their system is better; ours is a fraud.

The Swiss aren't the only ones we can learn from. The Asian tigers have tax systems that do not punish enterprise. The Taiwanese have a saying, "People will produce if they are allowed to keep the fruit of their labor." Japan's dominant political party has a basic premise that has maintained its popularity: "Economic progress is our primary goal." An ancient Asian proverb goes, "It is not the heavy taxed realm that executes great deeds but the moderately taxed one." These statements should sound familiar since they are so similar to the ideas of our founders; but we cannot accuse the Asians of copying from us. Their ideas go back many, many centuries, to the dawn of their written history. Lao Tsu, the revered founder of Taoism, wrote over 2,500 years ago:

> The more one governs, the less one achieves the desired result. . . . The more restrictions and prohibitions there are in the world, the poorer the people will be. . . . The more laws are promulgated, the more thieves and bandits there will be.

> When taxes are too high, people go hungry;
> When the government is too intrusive, people lose their spirit.
> Act in the people's benefit. Trust them, leave them alone.

> Governing a large country is like frying a small fish; you spoil it with too much poking.

But the best wisdom of the Chinese is found in this modern translation of an ancient text:

> The king was having a discussion with his spiritual adviser, and asked, "What should I do when my government does not have enough money to do all the important things?"
>
> The sage replied, "Use the ancient time-honored tax method of taking a tenth of the people's production."
>
> "Taking two-tenths is still not enough, not to mention one," said the king.
>
> Said the sage, "Decrease the tax, attract the people to till the land, and invest in your country. This means increase the revenue by decreasing it. When all the people have enough, the government has enough. . . . Too much tax is self-robbery in that it does not nurture the strength of the people to pay the tax."

This is good advice. We ignore it at our peril. Eschewing the mistakes and the wisdom of our predecessors, we walk blindly into bankruptcy. Can we redirect our steps?

18

The Rebellion of the Rich
(Patriotism Is Soluble in Taxes)

Single out the big and moderately big properties
for attack, and very soon, as if by magic, they will
begin to evade you and disappear, as all things in
the world very reasonably do when they are sin-
gled out for attack. Even the half-starved crow
will not wait to be continuously shot at.

—*The Times* (London), May 17, 1894 (when
progressive tax rates were adopted)

The current tax reform debate has renewed interest in the "fairness" argument. Those who oppose most tax reforms harp on the unfairness of taxes on consumption, reducing capital gains or estate taxes, or high income tax brackets. The prevailing belief is that the United States is a kind of tax haven for the wealthy and corporations—the rich and powerful don't pay much tax as it is, so any tax reform that shifts tax burdens away from the rich is ipso facto bad.

President Clinton used these arguments successfully to lobby his

1993 tax increases through the Congress—increases, so he said, that would only fall on the top 1.5 or 2 percent, who could easily pay more. The Democratic National Committee is still hammering away with a recent questionnaire sent out in 1995, with loaded questions like:

> "Republicans have proposed a 'new budget plan' which would provide large tax cuts for the rich . . ."
>
> "Do you favor or oppose Republican efforts to enact a capital gains tax cut which would deliver 70% of its benefits to households making more than $200,000 per year?"

The implication of these questions is that the tax reformers are out to benefit the rich at the expense of the average Joe.

Tax reformers have bungled the fairness debate by trying to dodge the fairness challenge. They emphasize the benefits of increased savings and capital formation, which would result in new businesses, improving old businesses, and making America more competitive in world markets. This would indirectly benefit the masses with more jobs from a growing economy, something tax dollars won't do. In short, a dollar in the hands of an enterprising capitalist is more beneficial to the nation than that same dollar in the hands of a federal bureaucrat. These are very legitimate arguments, but they sidestep the contention of the anti-tax reformers with their advocacy of soaking the rich.

The propaganda machine has done its job well. Just about everyone "knows" that the wealthy and corporate America get away with paying little tax, using huge loopholes in the tax system, while the poorer and lower middle classes get clobbered with taxes they cannot avoid. But the facts show otherwise.

Progressive taxation against the wealthy in America far surpasses any other country, including Sweden. Our corporate profits are taxed more heavily than in any other Western nation; our property taxes are the heaviest in the world, and they fall primarily on the rich; and for decades America has collected more taxes from estates and gifts than any other country. And as for the poor, our marginal income tax rates are the lowest in the Western world, where they usually start at 30 percent. Even a common item like annual automobile licensing is stacked against the rich, with fees based on the value of the car, while elsewhere all cars pay the same rate. So when Laura Tyson, President Clinton's first economic chief, claimed that America was an undertaxed nation, she was right if you look at the taxes paid by the lower-income classes.

When you get down to the nuts and bolts of the "fairness" argument, it is the rich who are getting clobbered with heavy taxes, if we compare ourselves with other high-tax Western democracies. Furthermore, it is not easy for the rich in America to avoid taxes, unlike the rest of the world. In other nations, the rich move to low-tax countries—but that won't work for Americans; the IRS follows them there. Our embassies abroad are all staffed with IRS agents hounding Americans for taxes, unless they give up their passports and wait ten years.

Except for the United States, income and death taxes are a residence tax—with every resident required to pay his or her share of the costs of the government that provides services and protection for the resident and his/her property. Once residency ceases, any moral justification for these taxes ends. But America is different, and exacts taxes like Louis XIV, the Sun-King of monarchical France. When one of his aides told him of the people's resentment of his taxes, he replied that all the wealth of his subjects was his, and when he took it he took only what belonged to him. Otherwise, how can you explain taxing nonresident citizens who take relatively nothing from the U.S. government, and pay taxes to the country where they reside, the country that provides the protection and services they enjoy? The moral duty to pay for those services and benefits is self-evident; but what is not at all self-evident is the rationale for paying taxes to a country you do not live in and which provides nothing—unless everything you own belongs to the U.S. government and, like Louis XIV, it only takes what be-

Whose money is Your Money?

longs to it. This is not as far-fetched as it may sound. Recently, President Clinton's latest Secretary of the Treasury, Robert Rubin, was asked about the injustice of the estate tax. He could see no injustice at all, in fact, the government was willing to let citizens keep some of their property—implying that the government could take it all if it wanted to. Specifically, the government takes at the 55 percent level, but could take the other 45 percent if it wanted to. Is not this Louis XIV's view of who really owns your property?

Many countries in worse fiscal shape than America, such as Canada, Australia, and New Zealand, have repealed death taxes as an unwise and unfair confiscation of capital and previously taxed income. The folly of capital confiscation was recently brought home to Angelenos when they learned their beloved Dodgers (the last family-owned major league baseball team) was up for sale. Peter O'Malley, the son of the owner, Walter O'Malley, said the confiscatory estate taxes were the culprit. The family could never raise or pay a 55 percent federal estate tax, so the Dodgers go on the auction block. And one more famous family business will end up in the control of a large public corporation, buying up another family enterprise so the family can pay an exorbitant tax bill.

Evidence unearthed about the impact of our death tax system on family businesses revealed that 90 percent of family businesses disappear after the founder dies because the family can't keep the business and pay the death taxes. When the big corporations take over the small business, jobs are lost. According to a George Mason University study by Richard Wagner, chairman of the economics department, 262,000 jobs alone have been lost since 1971 alone because of this disastrous tax. There is a public policy issue here: Is the survival of family businesses and farms as important as retaining a tax that confiscates much of a family's wealth at death? The answer, so far as Congress is concerned, is—family businesses and farms don't matter much. That is, the feds need the money more than the country needs family businesses and farms.

In most other countries capital gains are hardly taxed, like Japan, or are taxed at reduced (50 percent) rates. All in all, the United States is the last country a rich person would want to call home if preservation of wealth is at all important. However, the world's rich do come here; but only after our best tax professionals rearrange their affairs and put their assets and income beyond the legal reach of the IRS. They pay some tax, of course, but the vast bulk of their wealth has been dropped off on their way to the United States in their favorite tax haven. Today, that tax game is in trouble with recent (1996) tax legislation that reaches out to tax that "dropped-off" wealth, as it has been called. It's likely that many of the world's rich and famous who came to live in America will be leaving and looking for a new home. Many of them live in London or even in Switzerland, with moderate taxes to pay—again all very legal, and with the blessing of the new host country.

Rich Americans will soon learn that the nations of the world, and not just the Caribbean tax havens, will welcome them with open arms and tolerable taxes. It is strange indeed that a rich Englishman can leave England, rearrange his affairs, and come to live in New York, with a greatly reduced tax burden, and similarly, a rich American can leave New York, take up residency in London, give up his citizenship, and live in England with extremely moderate taxation. That's crazy, of course, but that's the way the world works for the rich. Wouldn't it be infinitely better if the American could stay in his country and the Englishman could stay in London, and both pay moderate taxes, rather than be forced to play this bizarre residency game?

How do the indigenous rich survive in America? Most have no choice but to set up tax-free foundations. The Ford and Rockefeller Foundations are the most famous, but there are many thousands more from less notable rich American families. Of course, they lose control, and the foundation is limited to spending for charitable purposes. The result is total tax avoidance on a huge bloc of wealth in the nation; but is this a wise policy? It deprives the Treasury of even a pittance at a time when some modest taxation would be beneficial to all and to the fiscal troubles of the nation.

The obvious objective of progressive taxation—soaking the rich—has turned against the advocates. In the end, the rich have disappeared "as if by magic." But worst of all, the middle classes have fallen into the ditch that was dug for the rich, just as the Russian proverb predicted.

Many of the rich have practiced the time-honored and ancient art of rebelling with their shoes. Today, that means transferring their wealth and often themselves to low-tax areas of the world. This is not limited to island tax havens offshore, like the Cayman Islands or Bermuda, but to many if not most of the advanced Western nations, who are happy to welcome our rich with tax holidays and reduced taxes. Residents of many of the world's tax havens read like a *Who's Who* among the world's rich. And for those not wanting to change residency, their wealth finds its way to a new low-tax home. A number of the world's governments are in intense competition trying to attract the wandering wealthy looking for a new home.

The only way to check this flight to the havens would be to do as the emperor Diocletian did around A.D. 300. He was faced with the flight of Roman taxpayers out of his system. He found it necessary to curb the freedom of travel of all Roman citizens—a freedom they had enjoyed for seven hundred years. The once free Roman was put in bondage to the tax collector to make sure taxes were not avoided through flight. Unless the high-tax nations of the world are willing to do as Diocletian did, wealth can easily take flight to low-tax countries. The other alternative is to require "exit permits," as the Communist states did, along with severe exchange controls.

There are a variety of exchange control systems, but in brief, exchange control requires approval from the central bank before the citizen can exchange his local money into foreign money, thus freezing his holdings in local currency. In effect, like Diocletian, it's your money that stays put, not your body. Margaret Thatcher will certainly be remembered for abolishing Britain's exchange controls.

There is no doubt that the flight of the rich to tax havens is harmful to any nation simply because of the revenue drain, but there is a brain drain and an enterprise drain that is far more serious. Adam Smith, in his *Wealth of Nations,* pointed this out as one of the bad consequences of too much taxation. The capital flight that accompanies the wealthy will mean lost jobs and lost business enterprises, noted Smith.

In America there has been a steady exodus of wealthy, fed-up, overtaxed citizens. But the burden of heavy taxes is not the only problem, and in some cases it is secondary. Many of the wealthy who have fled complain about an arrogant bureaucracy that hounds them for more money, perpetual tax audits that never end, and the threat of prison hanging over their heads; some have left for these reasons alone. Again, Adam Smith complained about this oppression as well, and in the 1865 article in *The Nation* about the Civil War income tax, the author points out that with respect to an income tax, "every one's business and mode of life is at the mercy of tax gatherers, who in all ages have been regarded as the most odious of mankind." Times have not changed.

John Templeton, of mutual fund fame, a native of Tennessee, left the United States in 1962, gave up his citizenship, and moved to Nassau. There he built a multistory building to house his staff and direct his investments and funds. The billion-dollar financial empire and support staff and industry he created could have been housed in the United States, with lucrative jobs for Americans. In 1992, when he sold his fund management business, his tax savings were estimated to be more than $100 million. When you add to that his enormous personal income, which is untaxed, and his estate that would soon be taxed, you are talking about a tax loss of at least $500 million, and that is just one taxpayer and one tax loss.

There was also John Dorrance III, heir to the Campbell's soups fortune—in the billions of dollars. Or, even more notorious, Kenneth Dart, heir to Dart Container and his family's billion-dollar fortune. He now operates out of the Cayman Islands with a Belize passport. In the manufacturing business there are those who have taken up Hong Kong citizenship, or Irish citizenship, and set up shop in those low-tax countries. Mr. Dorrance, for example, is carrying an Irish passport, and instead of facing a 55 percent confiscation at death by the IRS, his Irish death tax will be 2 percent.

When President Clinton pushed through Congress his 1993 tax bill by the narrowest of margins, supposedly to soak only the rich, 306 super-rich left the country and renounced their citizenship. In the end it was the upper middle class who were clobbered with in-

*This cartoon shows signposts giving the miles from
New York to some of the well-known tax havens.*

numerable tax traps, not the super-rich, who have always had the
means to avoid tax confiscations no matter how hard a government
tries. Perhaps the one exception was the Russian Communist revolution. They solved the problem by simply "exterminating the
bourgeoisie," after confiscating all their wealth. But a wasteland
was left in which there was no enterprise, no taxes, no private
property, only a new dark age that enslaved the Russian people.

America is not alone in this problem. The world's many tax
havens are flooded with super-rich looking for a new abode. They

are welcomed with open arms, along with their money, of course. Canada lost E. P. Taylor of horse-racing fame. He buddied with Templeton in Nassau's exclusive Lyford Cay, which he developed. The British have lost thousands of their rich and famous, such as Sean Connery, who also resides in the Bahamas, or the Rolling Stones. The Swedes lost their most famous tennis star, Bjorn Borg, and the skiing sensation, Ingemar Stenmark. Both reside in Monaco, where many of Europe's rich choose to live.

One of the tragic examples of a super-rich tennis star staying at home and trying to manage the taxman, unsuccessfully, was Steffi Graf. Her father took over her tax-planning chores and ended up in jail, while his daughter ended up with a huge tax bill. Consider how much easier it would have been if she had taken up residency in Monaco, like the other great European athletes—no tax, no jail, no hassle by Germany's tax thugs; in short, no problems.

Tax havens are like the biblical cities of refuge, now for the rich as protection from avaricious tax systems that seek to extort and plunder wealth. But these havens are not new. Overtaxed people have been fleeing to tax-free or low-tax climes since ancient times. America was the great tax haven for Europeans in the early modern period, and the United States, in its first 150 years, was a refuge from European taxes for most of its immigrants. Tax havens will go away when taxes become reasonable, moderate, and fair. If Bill Archer's national sales tax ever replaces the income tax, you can expect a wave of new immigrants, our rich and famous wanting to return to the USA.

19

"No One Can Steal from the State"

—French proverb

The French proverb above may come as a shock, yet it was very popular within the monarchy, probably because the tax law was without any principles whatsoever. It lacked uniformity in the most grotesque way. Today, this proverb wouldn't be treated very kindly by our government. IRS agents routinely speak of your tax money as belonging to Uncle Sam, which it does once you have paid it, but not before. You earned it; it is your money, unless, of course, you adhere to the Louis XIV view of your property. The converse of the French proverb is that "every state can steal from the people." So, to the French, turnabout seemed fair play.

Our government can steal from the people, and routinely does so, when taxes lack uniformity, just as in the Ancien Régime, and when the tax rates almost confiscate everything. Twenty years ago, the top tax rate for Sweden was 105 percent, and in Britain, 102 percent. Now, if that's not stealing, I don't know what is. British people in the top brackets had to plead with their bankers not to pay interest, for obvious reasons. In Sweden, the top rate was only 85 percent, but there was a 20 percent tax for employee benefits, which added up to 105 percent. In the United States, our government was not quite as thievish as were the Swedes or British, as our rate was only 91 percent. Some years ago, someone watching President Reagan playing golf noticed what a fine, accomplished golf swing he had, and wondered why. It was easy. As an actor in the days of our 91 percent income tax, Reagan would stop working about midyear and play golf for the rest of the year. There was no incentive to work and pay taxes in the 91 percent bracket.

Today, the 91 percent brackets are gone, but the total lack of uniformity prevails, so the thievery is still there, though on a less outrageous level. The Supreme Court has abandoned its role as guardian of the Constitution with regard to taxes and spending. Moreover, a significant number of taxpayers have manufactured a lot of strange arguments to support their contention that they don't have to pay these unprincipled taxes. They maintain that the tax law is voluntary (the IRS said so), and they conduct seminars around the country, and for a very substantial fee you can buy one of their packets of silly documents and construct your own personal Tax Reform Act. But their arguments are not any more ridiculous than those of the nine men and women in black robes telling us that the constitutional controls over taxation don't mean anything. If they don't mean anything, then why were they put there? I guess you can say that one bit of nonsense invites another.

Of course, these resisters can't win in the judicial arena, but every once in awhile they do win a criminal case of tax evasion. They claim that these victories prove you don't have to pay your taxes. What these cases really stand for is that if you sincerely believe the tax is unconstitutional or voluntary, then you lack criminal intent and are not guilty of tax evasion. This does not mean you don't owe the taxman. The civil tax liability, with interest and penalties, has to be paid.

Those genuinely interested in getting rid of the income tax or making a major overhaul, like the flat tax, have found these resisters more harmful than helpful. They offer no alternative other than complete national collapse. For, if the tax is not constitutional, then every taxpayer would be entitled to a tax refund for the past three years. (The statute of limitations bars the recovery of any unlawful tax after three years.) The U.S. government couldn't manage such a fiscal disaster. No court is going to make a ruling that would destroy the nation.

The argument that the tax is voluntary—that you don't have to pay it if you don't want to—is an absurdity too ridiculous to give consideration. A tax, by definition, is a forced exaction. If it is voluntary, it is not a tax. The few times the word "voluntary" is used in IRS publications, it really means that the system is self-assessing, taxation by confession. Most people know that, but there will be a few foolish tax rebels who will hang their resistance on any idea, however absurd.

There are three classes of tax resisters. There are those who deserve our admiration, in the tradition of Gandhi or America's Thoreau, or the Whiskey rebels of 1794 and 1865–1900. They pointed out evils that needed attention, especially taxes that lacked uniformity in substance. Karl Hess, whom we will discuss at some length, was such a rebel. But another class, those who fall back on the nonsense that a tax is voluntary, are of little value when it comes to correcting the tax mess that has been created.

There is a third group of resisters, including those in the underground, who are invisible. They don't rebel so much against the taxes as they do the spending. They see billions of dollars spent to benefit powerful special interests with political clout, and they don't like it. Adam Smith, in *The Wealth of Nations,* saw their problem clearly, over two hundred years ago: "When there is a general suspicion of much unnecessary expense and misapplication of the public revenue, the laws that protect it will not be respected."

Today, the vast majority of taxpayers know that a large part of their money goes for matters that do not benefit the general welfare, but rather some special welfare groups that have secured a seat at the public trough—welfare recipients, farm subsidies, corporate subsidies, local pork, entitlements, and expensive military hardware for an enemy long gone. And for every special welfare group that receives the taxpayers' money, there are a dozen or more clamoring to secure a seat at the trough. What most taxpayers are beginning to realize is an economic truth: whatever you subsidize, you get more of, not less. Give handouts to the unemployed and you get more unemployed; support teenage unwed mothers and you get more teenage unwed mothers.

There is the lesson Roman rulers learned when they gave free food and entertainment to Romans who chose not to work. At first, those who qualified numbered about 200,000, and the costs were paid for by the emperor and Roman and provincial taxpayers. Once word got out, the ranks almost doubled as peasant farmers came to Rome, gave up their farming duties, and joined the rabble. When Julius Caesar came to rule, he cut the number substantially through an ingenious device. He shipped thousands of the freeloaders to the provinces, where they would have to work— where there was no free lunch. But no emperor could ever get out from under this costly government handout. It contributed to the fiscal troubles of Rome in the centuries to follow, playing no small role in Rome's prolonged inflation, heavy taxes, decline, and eventual collapse.

To most taxpayers trying to make ends meet on their own, the government has got its priorities askew, and the average American can't help but see him or herself as the victim, and not the beneficiary of government spending. All they ask is to be left alone to work, raise their children, and be provided with a safe world in which to live. They don't want handouts, and they object to a government that can't say no to every hard-luck story that comes along and makes its pitch to the Washington spenders. But what they do want is a safe place to live, and they feel government has the duty to provide that, first and foremost.

Take a modest city like New Haven, Connecticut, which in 1960 had six murders, four rapes, and sixteen robberies, In 1990, when the city was 14 percent smaller, there were 31 murders, 168 rapes, and a whopping 1,784 robberies. Robberies increased by over 100 times. New Haven is not unique, the same story holds true for much of America. Milwaukee, in 1965, had 214 robberies, in 1990, again a smaller city, there were 4,472 robberies. Even though government expenditures have escalated, violent crime, real crime, has gone off the chart. Government has failed in its first duty, and that makes taxpayers angry and rebellious. What good is government if it can't protect one's life and property? Shouldn't the government forget handouts and clean out the vipers' nests of vicious criminals that are everywhere around us?

In the declining years of Rome and ancient Egypt, lawlessness was everywhere. The roads were filled with robbers in the Roman empire, and in Egypt even the Nile was no longer safe for travel as governments lost their will to protect commerce and citizens. Could we be on the same course? The crime statistics are shocking—are they the earliest warning signs of a declining nation, or even civilization?

John Locke, whose political ideas inspired the founders, noted "the preservation of property being the end of government." Similarly, Montesquieu said that taxes were that part of a person's property which he gave up in order to have protection in the part that remained. Today, where is that protection? Many are forced to live in walled and fenced compounds, with security police whom they must pay privately. What taxpayers are seeing is a "misapplication of the public revenue." Protection should come first. When that is achieved, some of the handouts can be considered. People want smaller government because big government has failed them in what counts most—protection from enemies within.

The shift from a national to a global economy has put tax reform, even rebellion, on a purely economic plane. This is perhaps the greatest threat of all to maintaining the present income tax system. It is the motive for lowering tax rates and reducing taxes on interest and capital gains—all of which discourage enterprise, increase costs of goods, and decrease America's competitive position in world commerce. Income taxes are a cost for making profits, no different from rent; a lower tax, or even no tax, means a lower cost for goods in commerce, hence a boon to American businesses in world markets.

Taxes brought about the decline of the Dutch empire, for the same reason. Because of high taxes on goods made in the Netherlands, British goods with lower taxes priced Dutch goods off the world markets. The great centers of Dutch industry went into decline. Leiden became a desolate town; its once flourishing cloth industry went into a depression. The linen industry in Haarlem had similarly shrunk. The products these centers once produced and exported could now be purchased abroad at lower prices. A modern Dutch historian explained the decline in simple terms: "War meant expense. Expense meant taxation. Taxation meant the strangling of trade."

In the 1970s and 1980s, rust belts began to develop in the giant industrial centers of America. Detroit, which was once the heartland for automobiles, had surrendered a large part of the American market to the Japanese—a market that was once almost an exclusive American domain. At the same time, all kinds of Japanese goods, especially electronics, found great favor with American consumers, at better prices. America was in trouble, for a time. But then Japan lent a helping hand—unwittingly, of course. In 1989, Japan instituted new taxes like a 20 percent withholding on interest income that had been tax free. Capital gains were taxed, and information returns were required. In short order, capital fled from Japan; with a loss in demand for Japanese securities, the stock market collapsed.

If this wasn't enough to injure what was called a "miracle economy," the once brilliant Japanese fiscal planners decided, unlike the other Asian nations, to yield to the temptation of central bank stimulation, and this set Japan on a boom-bust course. With Central Bank credits, Japanese banks were able to lend funds beyond what had been available from private savings, now subject to a 20 percent tax. The Central Bank then artificially pushed interest rates below market levels, creating an artificial demand for borrowing in all sectors. Prices soared, making a bust inevitable. Thus, thanks to the follies of the once economically invincible Japanese leadership, America was saved. The Japanese were forced to bring the manufacturing of their products, including their cars, to America, thus stimulating, rather than crippling the American economy.

But America is not completely out of the woods yet. To replace the Japanese we now face a host of Asian tigers, with China leading the pack. America will have to be constantly adjusting its tax system to keep its businesses competitive. Otherwise, we may end up like the Netherlands who were driven off world markets by lower taxed British goods.

What makes this great competitive struggle for world markets of historical interest is that the principles that have made America's rivals great were first introduced in the modern world by America. The motto of American society seventy-five years ago was, "The business of America is business." Today, that is the motto of our world competitors. It is hard to say what our primary business is. In the business world, if you ask foreign businessmen, they are likely to say it is the world's worst tax system, with tentacles from our tax octopus reaching around the world. No other tax system can make such a claim. The IRS has agents in every U.S. embassy to see that the U.S. tax law is enforced. No other government has revenue agents as permanent embassy attachés. We have them everywhere—the ubiquitous IRS.

Is our tax system really the worst? Some tax experts have challenged that assertion, because some nations have higher rates of tax for income or estates. That is so, but when you add all the negatives, America wins hands down. You can never judge a tax system by its rates alone. When Genghis Khan invaded Russia and destroyed most civilized life, he was only enforcing a 10% tax system—on everything.

Countries with higher rates can be found to have more loopholes—huge gaps through which income can flow untaxed. Take death taxes. America collects more than any other nation, no matter how you analyze it. Some countries have rates higher than ours, but very few qualify, since those rates apply to strangers who inherit wealth. Close family members like sons and daughters pay rates usually around 5 percent, never more than 20 percent. And what country locks its tax sinners up for over twenty-five years while bank robbers seldom get half that much? What does this mean?

There are three interpretations that I can suggest. First: everyone in the country is a crook, and to make the tax system work, you have to act accordingly—spy extensively on all economic activity and punish tax rebels the same as robbers, burglars, and killers. Second: our federal judges have a mean streak in them, like psychopathic Justice Samuel Chase (see Chapter 6). Third: Americans have always rebelled against bad taxes.

ONE OF THE TOOLS historians use to understand a nation is to look into its criminal laws. Not the laws of real crime, but of synthetic crime—manufactured by the state and coupled with savage punishments. When you burn witches to death, you obviously believe the irregular behavior of these women is a great danger to society. Or take the Soviet Union, and look at the long prison terms for anyone operating a small business against the will of the central planning bureaucracy. So, when America makes a crime of not paying your taxes—a crime that did not exist at Common Law—that tells the historian something. Especially in a society in which its greatest thinkers and philosophers condemned making tax evasion a crime. The U.S. government obviously feels terribly threatened by its citizens, a great number of whom would evade taxation if they could—people who are otherwise excellent citizens. Adam Smith said in *The Wealth of Nations* that evasion of taxes was a crime "nature never meant to be."

*The beloved humorist Will Rogers seen with Vice President John Garner.
Rogers captured American attention with his wise and witty comments about
the income tax, and his own problems with the IRB. He claimed a large de-
duction for his wife's services when about all she did was open the mail. When
he said the income tax made more liars out of the Americans than golf had, he
had himself in mind as much as anyone else.*

But why is the American taxpayer so prone to evade? Are we really that bad? Or does the badness rest with the tax system? Are we
rebelling with the same spirit and the same justification as the
farmers in western Pennsylvania in 1794? I think that is the answer.
We rebel in our own way, maybe unwittingly sensing our long historical right to do so. It means that the "sacred right of insurrection" that was so dear to the hearts of the founders is still alive and
well. It also means the rebellion won't go away until Congress reforms the system. As Jefferson said, the rebels are pointing out sickness the government needs to heal. The tax resisters, evaders,
protestors, all these rebels are giving a message to government, and
they deserve a fair hearing, not psychopathic punishments or ban-
ishment from American society.

In 1832, as we noted, Benjamin Oliver wrote a wonderful book
about America at that time, and its government—its good govern-

ment. But he acknowledged that it would be oppressive, as well as unconstitutional, to compel a taxpayer to pay more than his due proportion of the public revenue. A. hundred years later, as we will note, America's beloved Will Rogers said nearly the same thing. But how can anyone know what their proportionate share is? The system makes no such attempt. Its insanity and complexity makes most taxpayers believe they are getting ripped off, or, as Mr. Oliver said, they are victims of oppression, and in American history that has always justified rebellion.

What we are experiencing is a new breed of tax rebels. They don't lynch or tar and feather; they don't burn down IRS buildings; but they do rebel, nevertheless. And the ranks of the tax rebels include almost everyone. Nixon's tax return made the cover of *Time* magazine. The Clintons, soon after the 1992 election, coughed up substantial sums for taxes they should have paid. Newt Gingrich has his troubles with using tax-exempt foundation funds for political purposes. When you read or hear of someone convicted of a tax sin, you might recall the story of John Bradford (1550), who remarked while someone was being led off to the gallows, "There but for the grace of God, goes John Bradford." The government's attitude, of course, is in the "Oh, ye sinner!" category, and strangely enough, the press goes along with this, afraid to acknowledge that tax gamesmanship is a national sport.

20

Putting On a Friendly Face

When Chairman Mikhail Gorbachev won the Nobel Peace Prize, most of the world thought he would become a savior to the Soviet people—save them from totalitarian communism and become a popular elected head of state, respected at home as much as abroad. That did not happen. He offered the Russian people communism with a friendly face, and they wanted no part of it. They had had a bellyfull of that enforced system—its security police, its Communist Party big shots and party members forming an entrenched aristocracy enjoying the fruits of the labors of others; its prohibition against private property, its war on religion, its shoddy goods and services, its lack of freedom in just about every way. The people weren't buying Gorbachev's communism. Soon Gorby disappeared from the Russian scene and found himself on the Western speakers' circuit, making big fees along with the likes of Margaret Thatcher.

The taxman has been trying to put on a friendly face now for years, but everyone knows what is behind the façade. Most recently, the IRS decided to call taxpayers "customers." But an audit is still an inquisition, call it what you may. French taxmen, who lined up at the guillotine to have their heads removed in 1792,

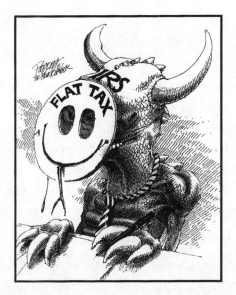

This interesting cartoon shows the IRS with a happy face, but behind the facade is an ugly dragon with a forked tongue, horns, and claws. The opponents of the flat tax believe it has a serious defect in not remedying a tax bureau that is out of control. This friendly face is not unlike Gorbachev's disastrous plan to give the Russians communism with a happy face. There were few takers.

could also be called customers of the executioner, but it would hardly have improved their dispositions for the few moments of life they had left. A national cartoon a few years ago showed a taxpayer on the phone with his accountant, urging him to end his audit ordeal as he was running out of tranquilizers. The problem is not with the IRS; they are no different from the headsman running the guillotine. It's their job, not their policy. The bad guys, for want of a better term, are the taxmakers, the men and women you vote for.

Getting rid of the IRS has been a political pitch made by many libertarians, even conservatives, wanting less government and certainly, most of all, less or no IRS. Ross Perot made the abolishment of the IRS one of his campaign pledges, and those favoring a national consumption tax point out that there will be no need for the IRS as we now know it. The problem is that all governments require taxes, and taxes require tax collectors. The bigger the government, the bigger the tax bureau has to be. But those in favor of a national sales or consumption tax are correct; a federal tax bureau, like our current IRS, will not be needed and will not intrude into every aspect of your life. Nevertheless, there will be taxmen, and it would be denying history to think they will have a friendly face.

Administration of the income tax in our times has had its many critics, but the tax resister whose harsh words were a sharp thorn in the IRS's side was the late Karl Hess, who called "the hollow men and women" of the IRS "the cold cogs of federal bureaucracy":

> Never has it come to my attention or been part of my experience that a revenue agent, a tax collector, has put humanity above regulation. They are, again in my experience, the most abjectly humorless, dehumanized, order taking, weak-charactered, easily vicious, almost casually amoral people I have met. If you want to look for a fascist's constituency in America, I would suggest that you . . . focus with prudential fear on the hollow men and women who are the cold cogs of federal bureaucracy such as the Internal Revenue System.

Karl Hess was Barry Goldwater's speechwriter. When Goldwater lost his bid for the presidency, Hess was audited along with the rest of Goldwater's staff. It seems one of the rights of the victor in a presidential campaign in those days was to audit the losers. Hess in anger withdrew from the Beltway, moved to West Virginia, and made his living as a welder, exchanging his services for the necessities of life. He continued to hammer on the IRS, so they went after him in the mountains of West Virginia. Two carloads of special agents showed up and seized everything in sight. They got nothing, only an angrier Hess, whose sharp pen became even sharper, as his words cut deep. Never has the IRS had such a formidable foe, who proved the adage that the pen is mightier than the sword. Karl Hess died recently, but his words will live as long as liberty lives in America.

NOTWITHSTANDING MR. HESS'S scathing indictment of the IRS and legions of complaints by taxpayers throughout the land, the IRS does not stand out as the only ghoul in the world's income tax administrations. The Gestapo is alive and well in Germany, housed in its tax administration. They shocked the head office of Merrill Lynch recently when an armed bunch of tax thugs showed up unannounced and seized carloads of company records, which they thought might contain evidence of tax evasion by Merrill Lynch's customers. But that was not all. They then arrested the staff and followed them home to search their houses in case records had been secretly kept away from the office. A lot of the non-German (American) personnel quit forthwith. The Gestapo of the Third Reich would have been proud, indeed.

Sweden has an anti terrorist law they use for tax investigations. They arrested their most famous film director, Ingmar Bergman, while he was making a movie, and took him down to tax head-quarters for questioning. He was so upset he ended up in a hospital and then fled the country into exile. It seems they had no case and he eventually returned. As part of that investigation they also arrested his most famous actress, Bibi Andersson, and took her in for questioning about Mr. Bergman. Her interrogation lasted for thirty-six hours, and she was not permitted to make one phone call, even to her teenage daughter who was home alone. She said, "They acted like Nazis." Another victim of Sweden's Gestapo tax system was the famous writer of children's books, Astrid Lindgren. She was ordered to pay an income tax at 102 percent. She then wrote an open letter to the tax bureau charging that there were hundreds of thousands of Swedes having heart attacks or turning into alcoholics, from wondering and worrying about how they could survive such crushing taxation. She didn't mention that many of Sweden's taxpayers may have been worrying about getting caught in Sweden's massive tax evasion underground.

Perhaps the most feared tax bureau of all is the *Okurasho* in Japan. That bureaucracy commands not only taxation but spend-

*Two victims of one of the twentieth century's ugliest tax systems
—author Astrid Lindgren and filmmaker Ingmar Bergman. Using
an anti-terrorist law, the Swedish taxmen have terrorized the people
with arbitrary arrests for purpose of interrogation—even for those not
under investigation.*

ing, banking, and the stock exchange. No publisher in Japan would
dare print anything critical, or even implicitly critical, of the
Okurasho. Foreign Affairs magazine, published in the United States,
called this tax ministry an "invisible Leviathan" with powers unthinkable in a modern democracy. Unlike the IRS, the *Okurasho*
manipulates Japanese politics from backstage.

America's friendly neighbor to the north found its tax bureau
out of control. In 1994, a government task force traveled around
Canada inviting taxpayers to come and air their complaints. Warren Beatty, the top taxman for the Canadian government, reported
in the *Toronto Sun* on April 8:

> We travelled the country to hear from taxpayers, business people, and
> tax practitioners. Each day brought a horror story worse than the day
> before—stories about people being forced out of business because they
> were made to pay money they didn't owe, stories of children's bank ac-
> counts being seized. . . . The tax system has become so complex and
> unfair that it drove people into the underground economy. . . .

The Canadian tax authorities and members of Parliament
should be commended for canvassing the country and hearing
from taxpayers. No congressional committee has done that in

America. They sit in Washington and invite witnesses, but if they really want to know how the IRS is working, they should also travel around the nation, from city to city, inviting taxpayers to come and tell their experiences. In short, the Ways and Means Committee needs to go to the people and hear firsthand what the tax people are really doing. If they went to Buffalo, New York, they might hear of the plight of a high school boy, whose only wealth was a bicycle. He exercised his right of free speech and wrote to the local newspaper complaining about the IRS, from something he had heard. The special agents in Buffalo read the article and assigned a number of these tax police to put the boy under twenty-four-hour surveillance. About the only thing they observed of interest was when he was in a drug store reading a girly magazine. They also put his mother under surveillance and followed her on the bus to work. Eventually, they called off the surveillance, and when members of Congress complained about this, the IRS refused to apologize—they were just doing their job of investigating all those who wrote or made negative comments about the tax bureau. Freedom of the press and free speech obviously does not include the right to criticize the IRS—and that is a well-known fact with the press.

Some years ago, the *Reader's Digest* published a series called "The Tyranny of the IRS." It shocked the country at the time, so much so that Congress held a hearing on the charges. The hearing turned out to be a total fraud. No one from *Reader's Digest* was invited to appear. The author was not invited, nor were the complaining taxpayers. In fact, there was only one witness, the Commissioner of the IRS, Sheldon Cohen. He said that the stories were filled with half-truths and should be ignored. The author responded to the IRS's account and made a further investigation of the facts reported by Mr. Cohen to the committee. It seems they tried to support the IRS's behavior by quoting from a federal judge who, it turned out, had made no such statement at all. Apparently this case stands for the proposition that lying to Congress does not apply to the IRS. To put this hearing in perspective: it would be like having only one witness at the Watergate hearings, with that witness being Richard Nixon. Why the whitewash? Why did the congressman go to such extremes to play ball with the IRS? The answer: Fear.

It is no surprise that the House Subcommittee for IRS Appropriations, which conducted the hearings on the *Reader's Digest* articles, licked the boots of the IRS. There is no member of Congress whose tax conscience is so clear that he or she is not afraid of the IRS. Times appear to have changed, fortunately. In the 1980s, a Democrat from Missouri, Senator David Pryor, successfully pushed through Congress, against the IRS's wishes, a "Taxpayer's Bill of Rights." At first, he could not find any House member courageous enough to co-sponsor the bill, but when it appeared safe to do so, just about every member of Congress got on the bandwagon, and the law passed.

In that era, the 1960s–70s, the IRS had already destroyed two senators who sought to hold hearings on IRS misdeeds, Senator Ed Long of Missouri, and Senator Joseph Montoya of New Mexico. Not long thereafter, they went after Congressman George Hansen of Idaho and destroyed his career after he wrote a book, *To Harass Our People*. Not playing ball with the IRS was dangerous to every congressman's political health.

Supreme Court justices have also felt the heavy hand of the IRS. William O. Douglas, the great dissenter, made it a point in his later years to dissent in all IRS cases, no matter what. He "dissented without opinion." Justice Douglas discovered, to his embarrassment, that information in his tax file had been leaked to the press, setting off demands for his impeachment. Even Gerald Ford went after Douglas, but Douglas weathered the storm. His "dissent without opinion" was his revolt against the IRS.

Justice Abe Fortas was not so fortunate. He had been on the Supreme Court for just four years, but had written some remarkable opinions. President Johnson nominated him for the job of Chief Justice, when Earl Warren was retiring. It seems the IRS had different ideas, so they had one of their agents meet with a reporter from *Life* magazine and give him embarrassing information from Justice Fortas's tax file. Fortas withdrew and even resigned from the High Court. No doubt the rest of the Court got the message.

These brief accounts of IRS misdeeds are merely the tip of the iceberg. If the entire nation was canvassed, the reports could fill a library. Recently, the IRS hired a historian, Shelley Davis, to collect and preserve the records of the IRS. When she tried to catalogue and record for history some of the IRS's past misdeeds, she found that many of the records had been destroyed. Eventually, the IRS turned on her. Special agents were called in to investigate her intrusions into the inner sanctum of the top brass. Ms. Davis had no alternative but to resign. Her story was recently published under the title *Unbridled Power, Inside the Secret Culture of the IRS* (1997). Davis was doing her job as a professional archivist. As it happened, her cataloguing threatened to vilify the IRS. Unsurprisingly, she was fired as a result.

CAN THE INCOME TAX be fixed? Can it operate in such a way that taxes are collected civilly? What's the remedy? Or is it beyond fixing? Frankly, its flaws are inherent in the system. That's why direct forms of taxation have been condemned throughout history. Remember, the Greeks believed tyranny was the consequence of the wrong kind of taxation—direct taxation. Have we not in the past century simply proven once again the wisdom and genius of the Greeks?

Charlie Rangel, the ranking Democrat on the powerful House Ways and Means Committee, says the IRS is unjustly maligned: "I'm sick and tired of politicians beating up on the IRS. We have the best and fairest tax-collection system in the world." When we hear from someone who knows better extolling the virtues of the IRS, I wonder if there really is any hope of reforming the system. Dan Rostenkowski, the former longtime chairman of the Ways and Means Committee, made similar comments, and he routinely took the IRS's side against critics. He even spoke out against the Taxpayer's Bill of Rights legislation, as the IRS desired. We now know why he was the IRS's man in Congress.

For real change to have any chance, tax laws should be scrapped and redrawn.

But the tax law is so complex, so unintelligible, that no one knows or can know if the system is fair. No one knows if he or she is paying the right tax, notwithstanding fairness. The income tax described by Will Rogers in the 1920s was a thousand times less complex, yet Will Rogers said, "When I pay my income tax *on-the-level,* I don't know if I'm a crook or a martyr." We must have a tax law that people understand, and also understand that it measures up to some degree of fairness. Take the sales tax. Everyone knows the rate, usually around 6–8 percent, and everyone knows there is no escape. We all pay, and the rate is the same for all. The same principle applies to customs and real property tax. The income tax is insane and has no principles, no visible fairness. About all that can be said is that it is the "Tax Accountants' Full Employment Act." It does create jobs, lots of them—over 120,000 with the IRS alone, and that many, many times over in the private sector. The system as a whole probably creates millions of jobs; how many we could never accurately calculate, but it reminds one of the Roman historian on the eve of the fall of Rome who observed that there seemed to be more people collecting and administering the tax system than there were taxpayers.

It is necessary to operate a spy system to make the tax system work. Espionage and massive surveillance is required not because Americans are all dishonest, but because no one believes the system is fair, and most taxpayers don't mind creating their own personal tax reform system. The concepts of tax evasion and tax avoidance have become blurred. Even the cartoons play games with the distinction. The IRS (page 207) is pictured as a Star Chamber, or Spanish-style torture inquisition, in this cartoon about President Richard Nixon's tax troubles:

By contrast, below is a fun cartoon, but no taxpayer would be-

"Aren't you the joker with the enemies list? . . . What an unexpected pleasure!"

lieve the IRS works this way. Audits are not like this, and don't expect an agent to make light of your tax sins in this manner. The cartoons on the following pages are at the other extreme.

Emerson wrote years ago that cartoons were often the truest

"First, the good news—You're in the running for our Chutzpah-of-the-month award."

history of the times. We find that especially true of tax cartoons, which contrast dramatically with tax editorials. Every March and early April, editorials come out in all the major newspapers and periodicals, urging people to pay their taxes honestly; at the same time cartoons come out like the ones above, which say in pictures what no writer would dare say in words. In addition, there are usually preplanned indictments that are put in the forefront, generally on the front pages, charging famous citizens with tax crimes and emphasizing how many years in prison they may have to serve, what we call in the law *ad terrorem*. Consider this subtitle to a March 24, 1997, tax article in *Forbes* magazine.

> The IRS has a new way to get ordinary decent folks to comply with the tax code: Throw other ordinary, decent folks in jail.

On the front page of the article is the picture of a lawyer, who says, "But I'm a nobody." He went to a federal prison camp for not paying his taxes on time. No fraud, no evasion, just derelict in his duty to pay when due. Lawyers and accountants are favorite targets, and there is a special division in the IRS just to punish tax professionals should they deviate from the IRS's bureaucratic line.

Charlie Rangel aside, in the polls that have been conducted, the vast majority of citizens believe that the tax system is not fair, is too complex, and needs a major overhaul. Since this is supposedly a de-

"Before we go over your return I'd like to read you your rights!"

"Congratulations, you have qualified for a rebate! But first a few questions . . ."

mocratic society that responds to the will of the people, why doesn't our Congress do what the people want? Why doesn't democracy work when the tax system is in disarray and disrepute? We will look into that when we explore the search for a just tax.

21

Yankee Ingenuity: The Tax Rebels Find a New Weapon

In the 1920s, Georges Clemenceau, the wartime prime minister of France, came to America to lecture at some of our major universities. As he was departing, he was interviewed by members of our press corps and asked about his impressions of America. Did he have any bad experiences, any criticisms to make? M. Clemenceau thought for a moment, and then answered, "Yes, there were a couple of matters. First, the Americans make a lousy cup of coffee; and second, they are appallingly ignorant of history."

Unfortunately, both those criticisms seem to be still true. Recently, our then secretary of state, Warren Christopher, and his cohorts testified before the Congress on why America should send troops to Bosnia for just a year. His historical analysis was so flawed, almost absurd, it is amazing that some member of the congressional committee didn't challenge him for his gross misunderstanding of our past involvements, such as sticking our nose into European affairs when we shouldn't have. And when it comes to taxes and history, our taxmakers are even more ignorant.

A few historians have called our leadership during the 1850s the

"Blundering Generation," for not working out the conflicts between the North and the South, and not averting the Civil War. But
that wasn't the only blundering generation that has left some bad
scars and long-lasting consequences we could do without. I am referring to the generation for the decade of 1913 to 1923. We could
use a new title for this group, such as "The Generation of Fools."

The first folly of this generation was to repudiate the wisdom of
the founders and adopt an income tax that had been prohibited by
the Constitution unless apportioned among the states. Then followed the first income tax law, which created unequal rates—progressive rates discriminating against the rich—and repudiated the
Constitution once again, tossing the uniformity command out the
window and shocking constitutional scholars.

The second fiscal folly was to get involved in the conflict among
Europe's great empires, battling for who was going to be top gun
in the world. For decades, German naval officers would make a
toast, "Der Tag," meaning the day they would take on the Royal
Navy. President Wilson thought the sacrifice of America's youth
was worth the price, "To make the world safe for democracy." Of
course, money is the heart of war, so the income tax system, which
was verbally guaranteed to never be more than a few percentages,
kicked into high gear to raise the funds necessary for the war. Rates
escalated from 7 percent to 77 percent to pay for the war. But a
strange thing happened. Instead of increasing revenues by 1100
percent, as the rates increased that much for the million-dollar
earners, the revenue collected was about the same at 77 percent as
it was at 7 percent.

Nine out of ten top-bracket taxpayers disappeared, as tax planning was born. In fact, high-income earners all the way down to
the upper middle class also began to disappear. Those with incomes
in the $300,000 range disappeared, though not quite as dramati-
cally as the million-dollar crowd; in the lower range, only four out
of five vanished. What is the explanation for this? I would call it
"Yankee Ingenuity." While tax planning is an international profes-

sion, nobody does it as well or with as much sophistication as the Americans, even to this day.

Yankee Ingenuity became the main tool of the tax rebels of the twentieth century. There were those who left the country, and there were those who created a cash economy. But by and large the primary pursuit of the new tax rebel was tax planning, and for every loophole the Congress tried to plug, a dozen more were discovered—some by virtue of knowing the right congressmen, and others by virtue of clever thinking.

Tax planning in its brashest form comes with having enough money and influence to have the tax law changed for your personal benefit. You can't be named for personal privilege—that would be totally unacceptable—but what you do is have a law designed to benefit you, and sometimes only you. One of the best examples of special tax legislation involved the movie mogul Louis B. Mayer, of MGM Studios. Mayer was about to receive a lump-sum retirement payment, taxable at 91 percent at that time. He was able to influence the right congressmen to pass a law called "Taxation of Employee Termination Agreements," which reduced his taxation to 25 percent, but which was so worded that only Mr. Mayer qualified. How's that for Yankee Ingenuity! The Supreme Court made this kind of ridiculous tax legislation possible by ruling that as long as the tax law is written in generalities, it meets the uniformity requirement. It is how it is worded, not how it operates, that is the constitutional question. Need I say, "How absurd!"

There is a never-ending flow of special tax legislation, usually for special groups like farmers, cattlemen, oilmen, certain types of investors, even businesses. These groups have promoters who gave rise to the name of a fascinating little book, *The Showdown at Gucci Gulch*. Now what does that mean? Gucci sells extremely expensive shoes. Only the very rich buy them, and in New York and Washington, D.C., that includes the rich lobbyists for special tax legislation. And where do they congregate? Outside the Ways and Means Committee. The "gulch" is thus the hallway outside the committee hearing room where these Gucci wearers linger to influence tax legislation for the rich and powerful.

Most Yankee Ingenuity takes place in the quiet of a tax professional's office. He studies the tax code and cases; he subscribes to many periodicals that zero in on tax loopholes, or he attends seminars and conferences where tax-avoidance techniques are explained, and then he or she runs back to the office and clients to put into practice some of the many tax gimmicks available.

Tax planning has its roots in taxes that are excessive and in the very nature of income taxation in a highly complex economic and fiscal society. Tax accountants like the law to be complex, as this increases the demands for their services. The IRS likes a complex tax law for job security because they feel that complexity increases the number of tax disputes. But tax professionals also like complexity because they, like their IRS opponents, believe complexity creates loopholes and thus permits them to win more cases. The 1986 tax law, which was promoted by the Reagan administration but which came from a Democratic Congress, was supposed to create a simpler tax law. We have heard that before, and we now know that complexity mushroomed, instead. One of our leading tax scholars, Boris Bittker of Yale University, examined this latest tax insanity, and concluded:

> I submit, therefore, that to a fee-maximizing tax professional, the Internal Revenue Code of 1986, as amended, is merely a platform waiting for energetic entrepreneurs to construct a superstructure of previously unimaginable complexity.

In other words, it is a gold mine for Yankee Ingenuity.

Finally, the third folly of this generation of fools was to think they could eliminate sin, which they were convinced was caused by John Barleycorn. Prohibition was made the law of the land by Constitutional Amendment, just as income taxation was made the law of the land. Prohibition, instead of getting rid of all sin, gave us Al Capone, organized crime, and gross disrespect for the law by the vast majority of citizens. Was not this a generation of fools, par excellence? We repealed Prohibition, shouldn't we also repeal the other folly of this generations of fools—the income tax amendment—and put these follies into the history books where they belong along with the Blundering Generation that gave us the Civil War?

22

The Search for the Just Tax

Whoever hopes a faultless tax to see,
Hopes what ne'er was, is not, and ne'er shall be.

—Alexander Pope, 1750

In this final chapter let us reflect upon the great tax debate of the 1990s, one that is bound to continue for years to come. Tax systems seem to have a life cycle of sorts. A tax system in its old age or senescence is despised by the populace, oppressive in administration, riddled with regulations that cripple commerce, and ready for the junk heap. Lack of popular respect as well as support sets the stage for its demise. In this period of decadence, a healthy state will bounce back with a new tax invention and give new vigor to a declining society. This did not happen during the decline and collapse of Rome, Imperial Spain, and even the great Netherlands empire, all of which were brought down, in part, by corrupt tax systems.

The time for a new tax invention is at hand, and all kinds of tax ideas—some good, some bad, some even crackpot—have been

Adam Smith, author of the four signs of a bad tax system

proposed. Every tax guru and expert has his or her own pet plan to save the nation. Ours is, in short, a time of searching for a just tax, even a faultless tax.

What are the "faults" of a bad tax system? Adam Smith, the founder of modern economics, in his great classic *The Wealth of Nations,* gave us four signs of a bad tax system, a system that is detrimental to the wealth of a nation:

First, a tax is bad if it requires a large and expensive bureaucracy to administer it. We can add to Smith's insight that a tax is similarly bad if it places heavy compliance costs on the taxpayer. Our tax bureau costs about $7 billion a year to administer at the government level. For the taxpayers, the costs have been estimated at between $300 and $600 billion, almost as much as half of the entire federal budget. Consider one example: Mobil Oil's tax counsel testified before the Ways and Means Committee that "It takes Mobil fifty-seven man-years at a cost of $10 million to prepare its income tax returns." To prove his point, he brought along to the committee hearings a stack of tax returns, four feet high, which weighed seventy-six pounds.

Second, a tax is bad that discourages enterprise, hard work, and investment—in Adam Smith's words, a tax that "may obstruct the industry of the people, and discourage them from applying to certain branches of business which might give maintenance and employment to great multitudes." In other words, it costs jobs. By taxing too much, said Smith, you take away the funds necessary to create new businesses and employment.

Third, a tax is bad that encourages evasion, and puts "an end to the benefits which the community might have received from the employment of their capitals." It is also wrong for government to create a temptation to evade, and then to punish the tax evader for yielding to the temptation.

Fourth, a tax is bad that puts people through "odious examinations of the tax-gatherer, and exposes them to much unnecessary trouble, vexation, and oppression." In other words, if it is direct. Any system that taxes citizens directly—their income, their wealth, etc.—is worse than one that taxes transactions. If the IRS audits a business to check sales taxes, that is more readily borne than if it audits individuals.

IT IS, SAID Smith, "in some one or other of these four different ways that taxes are frequently so much more burdensome to the people than they are beneficial to the sovereign." Note that Smith said one of these is enough to make a bad tax system. In our case, we have all four. Today's reformers will fail if they do not heed Smith's advice.

Today, the leading contenders for reform are the flat tax and various alternatives to the income tax, such as a tax on consumption, or a value-added tax. Congressman Dick Armey leads the flat tax brigade and the chairman of Ways and Means, Bill Archer, is for getting rid of the income tax. Not everyone is a reformer, of course. Lee Samuels of the Treasury was President Clinton's witness at the recent hearings on getting rid of the income tax. Samuels said the White House liked the tax system "just the way it is." Even Democrats winced. In 1816, the British government was shocked when Parliament threw their income tax out the window and burned all the tax records. When it comes to taxes, governments have a tendency to be removed from the temper of the people.

The flat tax has its defenders, since income from interest and capital gains and dividends is all tax-exempt, and would act as a strong incentive for capital formation. Japan's rate of capital formation has been nothing short of miraculous, a rate unknown in world history; tax exemption for interest income, and extremely low capital transfer taxes, have been major factors. Recently, as we noted, the Japanese started taxing interest and some capital gains, and shortly thereafter their stock market collapsed. Following Western tax practices may not have been such a good idea. But those who admire the great capital formation by Japan over the past decades point out that the Japanese do not have a long tradition of savings. In the 1930s, their savings rate was the same as ours, but tax policy changed all that. The proposed flat tax might bring about a similar result in the United States.

Consider, however, the matter of exemptions and burdens of the flat tax. An ideal flat tax would have a single tax rate that was the same for all income levels, making it "common to all," as the founders desired at the Constitutional Convention. Exempting income taxes from—interest, dividends, and gains—may have some economic merit in capital formation, but it strikes a negative chord for tax equity.

GLADSTONE SALVE—FOR TENDER CONSCIENCES.

" *The inequalities and anomalies of the Income Tax have this advantage; namely, that* THEY ARE UNDERSTOOD. *The back leans in adapt itself to the burden.*"—Speech of MR. GLADSTONE in the House of Commons.

THE MEANING.—" *I mean, of course, that as a man* QUITE UNDERSTANDS *that the tax is unequal and anomalous, he adapts the burden to what he considers the powers of his back.*"—Literal Translation by MR. PUNCH.

☞ The injustice of the Income Tax assessment, whereby precarious incomes are charged at a similar rate with assured incomes, has not yet been remedied.—1863.

The British magazine, Punch, in 1863, ridicules Gladstone, who condemned flat tax rates for *precarious* income (i.e., wages) vs. *assured* income (interest and return from capital), but did nothing to remedy the law's injustice. This caricature bore the caption: "GLADSTONE SALVE—FOR TENDER CONSCIENCES . . . The imposition of the Income Tax assessments, whereby precarious incomes are charged at a similar rate with assured incomes, has not yet been remedied."

A hundred years ago in Britain, a debate raged for decades over their flat tax:

The equitable issue was simple. A person's earnings are precarious. A job may end abruptly; sickness, old age, and any number of factors can put an end to one's wages; but the income from investments is not subject to such precariousness. It would be *assured,* argued the critics, although that ignores the question of risk and shifting returns on investments. But the conclusion of the critics was that wages should bear a lower tax rate than income from capital.

Proponents of the new flat tax proposal will argue that interest payments are no longer deductible, and the same is true for dividends which bear tax at the corporate level. But the average wage earner who has little "assured income" will deride any income tax system where the rich guy doesn't pay any visible tax on his investments.

The second most serious flaw, which may not be repairable with any income tax reform, is that flat income taxes are classified as direct taxes, which have been condemned for 2,500 years. Direct taxes make people slaves, wrote Montesquieu, and this is what Adam Smith's point number four had in mind. Look at our income tax today: doesn't the IRS operate a spy system? Fiscal privacy is almost nonexistent. Tax punishments are savage and even arbitrary. The current tax revolt means taxpayers have had enough of a tax bureaucracy that is out of control, in which millions of people, both guilty and innocent, suffer needlessly and extensively at the hands of taxmen who have powers reminiscent of the worst tax bureaus in history.

The flat tax, however, still might end up as the tax most likely to replace our current internal revenue system. There have been some brilliant economists who have taken the Armey plan—which they deem badly flawed—and have worked the bugs out of the system, especially the apparent injustice to the little guy, even the middle class. For example, besides the fact that wages are taxed, and capital income is not, payroll taxes continue for the wage earner. And a majority of working people pay more in payroll taxes than they do in income tax. That needs to be addressed as well. If the flat tax is to become viable, the proponents will have to listen to some of the positive constructive criticisms and solutions, like those proposed by the Washingtonian think tank of Lehrman, Bell, Mueller Cannon, Inc. They have answers for the flat taxers.

Many reformers feel that the object is to replace the income tax,

Arab, Irish, and American Terrorists.

not reform it, to "tear it out by its roots," as Chairman Bill Archer proposed. His analogy of comparing the income tax to a noxious weed that grows back is based on his experience as a legislator for over twenty-five years. Every time they reform the income tax— make some positive improvement—the ugly weed grows back. So, you do like any good gardener, you tear it out by its roots. Over the past twenty years, Congress has made dramatic rate reductions from 70 percent down to 28 percent in 1986; but then, with no reduction in expenditures, the rates have moved back up to about 40 percent, with a significant number of tax-saving provisions blocked, and capital gains higher than ever. The 1997 tax law pruned back some taxes and tax rates, but how long will they last? It is easy to agree with Chairman Archer that the noxious weed grows back no matter how often you cut it back. History proves Mr. Archer is right.

What about Mr. Archer's plan? As chairman of the powerful Ways and Means Committee, he is in a position to do something about genuine tax reform. First, he is not a dogmatist—he is not locked into any fixed tax reform plan other than to get rid of the income tax. He has proposed a national sales tax, and there are many groups who support this idea, as well as some of our recent Republican presidential candidates. First, and most important, this most ancient form of taxation will satisfy the no-direct-tax advocates, the libertarians, and those who believe the lesson of history that direct taxes produce tyranny and that indirect taxes are most compatible with a free society. Unlike most state income tax systems, a national sales tax that replaces an income tax will have a much broader base—it will tax service income, like your car repairman, your accountant, even your dentist, exempting, however, small enterprises.

What is nice about this plan for the average working person is that withholding taxes are gone. This means that most wage earners will have hundreds of dollars added to their paychecks. No more tax returns, and for just about everyone, no more IRS in your life. Mothers won't have to withhold taxes from their baby-sitters, fearing going to jail if they don't. But again, some adjustments and exemptions will have to be brought in to make it acceptable to the poorer classes. There will be a great loss of taxmen. The IRS will have to let tens of thousands of agents go. No tears will be shed for ridding society of those sharks. And in the private sector, perhaps a million tax professionals will have to find other employment, something more beneficial to society. It is a sad event when our brightest students gravitate to the tax world, where the income is the highest. Their intelligence could be put to real, productive work.

THE MOST POPULAR consumption tax format in the world today is the VAT, or value-added tax. It was invented in Europe for the European Economic Community (EEC), and all member countries are required to have this form of taxation. It was an ingenious device to deal with the cross-border problem with sales taxes. That could have crippled trade within what was to be a free trade economic community. It has worked well for Europe and recently has spread throughout most of the industrial world—Japan, Switzerland, Canada, New Zealand, and so on. But it is not used in the United States, where it has been vociferously attacked. It is, to its American opponents, just plain bad. But if it is so bad, why has just about every industrial advanced nation adopted a VAT?

First, as a tax on consumption, it has taken the pressure off the income tax and death tax systems, supposedly to permit a reduction in tax rates, and even a repeal of death taxes entirely. Critics have pointed out that the reductions have not always happened. In Canada, for instance, the tax turned out to be hated by the people, as income taxes did not make any dramatic move downward. New Zealand handled the matter more sensibly, perhaps brilliantly. The income tax was cut in half, with only two graduated steps. Next, they cut the income tax many weeks before their VAT (Goods and Services Tax) became operative. This greatly increased the take-home pay of workers, who quickly became converts to the tax reform. Within a year there was a new election and the incumbent party won an overwhelming majority. The people liked the new consumption tax with a dramatic reduction in income taxes.

Here's how the VAT works and how it differs from an excise or sales tax: Take the shoemaker who buys leather and supplies to make shoes. Suppose he pays $100 for these supplies and then sells his shoes, the finished product, for $175. He has added only $75 of value to the raw materials, hence he is taxed on that value added only, not the full $175. This is unlike an excise tax, which would be a tax on the full amount, and then the retailer could be taxed on the full amount again.

Continental Europe has had centuries of affinity with excise taxes, unlike America, where they have been hated since before the revolution. It is only to be expected that the Europeans have worked out an ingenious and workable excise that does not cripple trade as did so many excise taxes in Europe's past. While many political leaders in America, like Newt Gingrich and Bill Clinton, have expressed an interest in the VAT, that interest disappears quickly when the wrath of the anti-VAT establishments unleashes its verbal rage on the proponent. It is in academia that VAT proponents can be found; but they don't have to get elected, and nobody listens to them anyway.

Maybe someday in America a rational debate over the VAT can take place and its merits truly be evaluated. Its superiority over a sales tax is that it is self-policing—making tax evasion far more difficult than with a sales tax—and that today it has almost universal acceptance in the world.

ONE INNOVATIVE GROUP in Florida has a tax plan called Just-One-Tax, what they call a Commerce Tax, and they cite Alexander Hamilton in *The Federalist, No. 12* as support. Said Hamilton:

> The ability of a country to pay taxes must always be proportioned, in a great degree to the quantity of money in circulation and to the celerity [speed] with which it circulates. Commerce, contributing to both these objects, must of necessity render the payment of taxes easier and facilitate the requisite supplies to the treasury.

Hamilton never had his commerce tax tried, and the few taxes that he did foster destroyed the Federalist Party in the process. But this novel tax idea would put a tax on the flow of money for all goods and services—the basis of our commerce. Since over $1 trillion moves each day, these tax reformers maintain that a modest tax of less than 1 percent would more than adequately finance government. Also, the collection would be indirect, eliminating the evils of direct income taxation. The idea may be easy to implement, given our computer world. It deserves consideration; though, again, it sounds too good to be true.

While this may come as a shock to the reformers in their

search for a single just tax, history suggests that it is unlikely any single tax can fill the needs of the nation, or measure up to the ethical demands of a just tax system. Alexander Hamilton would be the first to object to a single tax solution for our revenue needs and problems. In *The Federalist No. 35* he argued against a single tax, such as an excise or import duties. Invariably, he said, a single tax will overburden some segment of society and underburden others. Hamilton argued that when great revenues are needed, as will sometime happen, a single tax will produce such a high rate that it will hurt commerce and foster evasion. Better to have a number of tax possibilities to spread the burdens and keep the rates moderate.

The tax historian learns one lesson above all: pragmatism. There are a few tax reformers who have suggested what Hamilton had in mind. Take the Princeton Economic Institute in New Jersey. The thinkers there want to abolish the personal income tax, but leave a corporate income tax at a flat 15 percent. They want a 10 percent national sales tax; a 10 percent increase in gasoline excise taxes; and a 2 percent national retail sales tax on real property transfers. They would end capital gain and estate and gift taxes. Social Security would be taken off the budget and managed as it was intended—as a trust fund where the funds can be invested.

These proposals, claims the institute, do not shift the tax base from capital to the working class. In effect, they want a middle ground between the two. They would broaden the tax base, not shrink it as so many single-tax ideologues end up doing. If they want an even broader tax base, they might add a 10 percent withholding tax on dividends, interest, rents, and royalties, making an indirect income tax like what was so popular in Britain in the nineteenth century. Japan's recent shift from tax-free interest to taxable interest involved a 20 percent automatic withholding, which was no doubt a fiscal shock to the thrifty Japanese. But this kept the tax system indirect so that the majority of Japanese do not have to file tax returns.

What About Super-Majorities?

The founders liked the idea of "super-majorities," which simply means that taxes cannot be adopted unless you have more than a majority of votes by legislators. In the Articles of Confederation, a super-majority of 75 percent of the states had to approve new taxes. Today, some state constitutions are being amended to require a super-majority, usually less than 75 percent, however.

But at the Constitutional Convention in 1787, we noted that the framers were willing to let a simple majority approve taxes and spending, akin to the British system. However, they then put checks and controls in the Constitution to prevent a simple majority from oppressing a minority group. First, taxes had to be initiated by the House of Representatives, which at that time was limited to taxpayers' representatives. No one could vote who was not a taxpayer. Then taxes had to be uniform—common to all and equal, as they explained their intention. Direct taxes needed an additional control—they had to be apportioned among the states. And if that wasn't enough, they then restricted tax expenditures, limiting them to defensive wars (no aggressive wars), and to matters that would benefit the nation as a whole. In other words, no pork. It was a brilliant plan, but it didn't work. Over time, the federal government circumvented these controls, and the states stood by and did nothing. Maybe we need to go back to the founders' idea of a super-majority check on taxmaking, and even spending, because we can't trust our federal government to follow the commands of the Constitution.

What About the Separation of Powers?

Looking back into history, whenever the power to tax and the power to spend reside in the same political body, be it a king, a congress, or an aristocracy, the power to spend will always overpower the power to tax. Governments will inevitably spend too much. They will always adjust their spending to their appetites, not to their wallets. They will debase their coinage, if necessary; steal from helpless minorities; and create enormous debts that will be passed on to future generations. They do not have the will to do otherwise.

The solution will always be found in the separation of powers, as in England in the early modern period when the king could spend but not tax, and Parliament could tax but not spend. That is the essence of what the separation of powers should mean.

Looking back into history for guidance, the historian as a tax reformer inevitably becomes pragmatic. He knows that most great nations and empires taxed themselves to death. He also knows that many great nations became great because of good, sound revenue systems, so the challenge is to single out the positive lessons from the past. Perhaps the best example of tax wisdom and of a reasonably balanced tax system is what made Great Britain a superpower in the eighteenth and nineteenth centuries. It was, strangely, a system not created by design, but by a series of uneasy compromises with rebellious British people.

The basic philosophy of the wisest of Britain's taxmakers was expressed by Henry Fox in 1748 after Robert Walpole's attempt to substitute excise taxes for import taxes produced a major tax revolt, even though the rates were the same. Henry Fox could have been prime minister at this time as he had been prominent in the government and a leader in the House of Commons, especially in tax policy. Said Fox in a speech on the floor of the House:

> All government must have a regard not only for what the people are *able* to bear, but what they are *willing* to pay, and the manner in which they are willing to pay, without being provoked to a rebellion.

The British system had a modest excise, but no general excise as on the Continent. A limited number of goods were taxed. They had duties on imports. There was a commerce tax in the form of stamp duties, essentially for items that otherwise missed taxation. There was a land tax, but the rates were low; and finally, there was a house-and-window tax for buildings, which exempted small dwellings for the poorer classes. All in all, these five major taxes reached the wealth of the nation without unduly burdening anyone. What is remarkable is that the ruling classes were not exempt, as was the case in so many nations on the Continent, where the poorer classes were heavily taxed. Also on the Continent, the excise was dominant, which crippled trade and gave Britain a powerful advantage in world markets. Even at the height of its empire, in the nineteenth century, the peacetime British income tax was a single digit, a modest rate, never more than 5 percent.

Britain's superior tax wisdom (like our own) did not last. As the twentieth century developed, Britain became seduced by socialism. The government abandoned the spirit of moderation in taxation and frugality in expenditures. It set the stage for Britain's decline into a third-class commercial power.

In our search for a better tax system, the wisdom of the past needs to temper the needs of our times. Pragmatic compromises may be necessary to avoid rebellions. To placate workers, for example, rather than a protective tariff, we could consider a modest sales tax on foreign goods, such as Canada has instituted.

If we use history as a guide for a better tax system, we would have to start by developing a tax system based on experience and principles of tax justice. Justice is not hard to articulate: Wealth should be taxed once only, and then moderately at most, lightly at best. All wealth, labor included, should pay its share of the cost of maintaining the common government. Even in ancient Rome, widows and orphans paid their small mite, and their contributions were set aside to provide uniforms for the cavalry. Interestingly, taxation was as much a right as a duty. Only citizens were permitted to pay. When our first income tax was adopted, there were many tax-exempt Americans who paid the base tax, even though they didn't have to do so. They felt that they had a duty to contribute to the costs of running the government they loved and that provided for them. No one seems to think like that anymore.

No tax is good if it is excessive. The Bill of Rights prohibits excessive fines; why not prohibit excessive taxes? Why is it that the criminal has such protection but the taxpayer does not?

In our search for the just tax system, no matter what path we may take, this simple observation by Will Rogers should be the objective of all taxmaking: "People want *just* taxes more than they want *lower* taxes. They want to know that every man [and woman] is paying his proportionate share according to his wealth."

Twenty-five-hundred years ago, a Greek general, Aristides, was enlisted to develop a tax system, as Will Rogers suggested, by assessing everyone according to what they were worth: "He drew up a list of assessments not only with scrupulous integrity and justice, but also in such a way that all states felt they had been justly and fairly taxed. . . . This levy of Aristides was a golden age for the allies of Athens."

The Greek story took a tragic turn. Aristides died, and the principle of tax justice died with him. Tax rates for Greece's allies were doubled, and then doubled again. The city-states in the Athenian League wanted to withdraw from the league and its crushing taxation. But Athens wouldn't let them out, and those city-states that tried were crushed by the Athenian legions and naval forces. The men were put to death for their tax defiance, and the women and children were sold into slavery. The rebelliousness of the rest of the city-states in the league weakened Athens' military forces and they were defeated by Sparta. The great Greek civilization declined and vanished from history. If only the government of Athens had followed the example of tax justice instituted by Aristides, the history of the world would have been different.

There are certainly parallels between America's tax history today and what happened after Aristides. Our taxes have doubled, and then doubled again. Many want out of the system, and many have rebelled and faced extreme punishments. Like the Athenians who

instituted the crushing taxation that brought about Greece's decline, our taxmakers won't listen to those in our past who stood for
tax justice and fair play. Would that our Congress could act with
the integrity of an Aristides, or of our founders, in taxmaking—
what the American people have longed for since the revolution,
and what our tax rebels have been fighting for.

FINALLY, WE BEGAN this journey through our history with some
shocking and apparently anti-tax words from *The Atlantic* magazine
in the late nineteenth century. The reader should not take that to
mean our forebears were anti-tax. They were not. They were against
excessive taxation, but they were very much in favor of wise and
moderate taxation, which they believed would be of great benefit to
society. We don't like bad taxation, either, but we look upon it as an
irritation, while they looked upon it as a calamity. This comment
from a March 1862 article, also in *The Atlantic* magazine, expresses
their view: "Introduce a wise and efficient system of taxation, and
life and energy will pervade the country. Without such a system, it
will sink into general and fatal paralysis." Again, as I said in the in-
troduction, you don't find statements like that anymore.

Most of those in charge of the public purse today, like our
learned president, tell us no nation ever suffered from heavy taxation, and our prosperity has nothing to do with low taxes. The
government's main purpose is to tax and tax, and spend and spend.
The bigger the spending pot, the better for everyone. If the president and his kind are right, then we can continue on our present
tax and spending binge with no fiscal problems. But if they are
wrong—and our forebears were right—then we will end up like so
many empires of the past that taxed themselves to death. Tax reformers today should focus on that question, most of all.

Suggestions for Further Reading

Part I. The Tyranny of British Taxation, 1764–1776

The importance of the Dutch, British, and French tax systems for the Americans up to the time of the Constitution can be understood by studying the chapters on those tax systems in my book, *For Good and Evil: The Impact of Taxes on the Course of Civilization* (Madison Books, 1993), chs. 21–26.

The British point of view was amply presented by Samuel Johnson in *Taxation No Tyranny* (1775). That view contrasts with the idea that consent to taxation had to be genuine and more than just the will of parliaments. See John Phillip Reid's remarkable study, *Constitutional History of the American Revolution*, Vol. II, *The Authority to Tax* (1987).

Part II. The Tyranny of Federalist Taxes, 1791–1799

There are many books on the Whiskey Rebellion, usually in support of the militant action taken against the rebels, but recent scholarship has challenged that view. See Thomas P. Slaughter, *The Whiskey Rebellion: Frontier Epilogue to the American Revolution* (1986), pp. 199–228; Bernard A. Weisberger, "Seeking a Real Tax Revolt," *American Heritage,* vol. 42, no. 2 (May–June 1991).

To understand the Fries Rebellion and the zeal of John Adams' cabinet to put Fries to death, as well as the efforts of the psychopathic judge Samuel Chase, examine the primary sources of the trial and rebellion in *The Tree of Liberty: A Documentary History of Rebellion and Political Crime in America* (1986), pp. 91–97.

Part III. The Tyranny of the Tariff, 1828–1861

With an estimated 70,000 books and articles on the Civil War, where does one start when looking for the tariff issue? Kenneth Stampp, a scholar of northerly persuasion, almost unwittingly provides an abundance of material pointing to taxation as the real force that set off the war. Examine *And the War Came: The North and the Secession Crisis* (1950). Against the hundreds of books deifying Lincoln and his noble cause, anyone seeking a balanced account should read John Shipley Tillery's *Lincoln Takes Command* (1941; reprinted 1991), and Edgar Lee Masters' *Lincoln the Man* (1930). A 1994 treatise, *The South Was Right,* by James and Walter Kennedy, should take the moralistic zeal out of anyone espousing the virtues of the northern invasions of the South.

My own article on how the British saw the Civil War can be found in "The Second American Revolution: The British View of the War Between the States," in *The Southern Partisan,* vol. 14 (1st qtr., 1994), pp. 16–20; "The 'Other' Great Debate, John Stuart Mill vs. Charles Dickens," *The Southern Partisan,* vol. 16 (3d qtr., 1996), pp. 27–34. My views are documented at some length in *For Good and Evil: The Impact of Taxes on the Course of Civilization* (1993), "Was It Taxes, Rather Than Slavery, That Caused the Civil War?" pp. 323–37. A recent book of real scholarship, a must read, is Jeffrey Hummel's *Emancipating Slaves, Enslaving Free Men* (1996). For a short, concise view of the war, see Doug Bandow's "Blame Lincoln for War He Could Have Averted," *Washington Times,* Feb. 17, 1996, p. E3.

Part IV. The Tyranny of the Revenuers, 1865–1900

Wilbur R. Miller's *Revenuers and Moonshiners* (1991) is a gem, without which this chapter could not have been written.

Part V. The Tyranny of the Income Tax, 1913–199?

Professor Edwin Seligman's 1911 classic, *The Income Tax* (reprinted 1970), did much to promote the Sixteenth Amendment and income taxes in America. His view was that the income tax would be quite compatible with a free society, and fears of runaway tax rates (over 5 percent), or totalitarian administration (like what was happening in Germany), would never happen here—the American people wouldn't stand for it! So, reasons Seligman, "What are we waiting for?" This remarkable work of research and scholarship is an example of a great scholar whose brilliant historical analysis and advocacy is only surpassed by the stupidity of his predictions.

The tyranny of the income tax is documented without any partisanship in David Burnham's *A Law Unto Itself: Power, Politics and the IRS* (1989). Couple this with Congressman George Hansen's *To Harass Our People: The IRS and Government Abuse of Power* (1980). On the real economic burdens of the income tax, examine James L. Payne's *Costly Returns* (1993). As with the Civil War, there are many hundreds of books on the evils of the income tax, with books and articles coming out every month, except during March and April, when journalists change their tune and admonish everyone to pay their taxes like Sir Lancelot, with a heart that is pure.

To get a good analysis of why progressive taxation is on shaky ground, Walter Blum and Harry Kalvern, Jr., laid out the problem in *The Uneasy Case for Progressive Income Taxation* (1953); also 25 *Yale Law Journal,* 427 (1916). A rather sobering read about the IRS is *The April Game* (1973), written by a former IRS agent who hides behind the pseudonym "Diogenes."

Index

235